C000135837

CHARACTER EVOLUTION

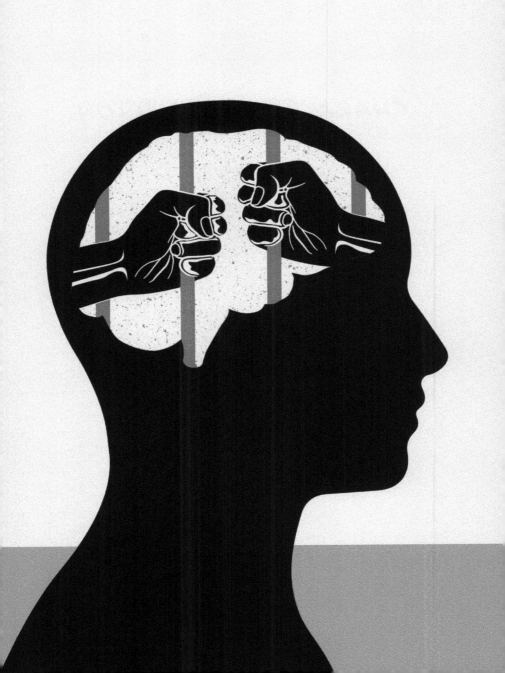

CHARACTER EVOLUTION

UNLEASH YOUR POTENTIAL.
EMBRACE GROWTH.
TRANSFORM YOUR JOURNEY.

ADAM HOLBROOK

CHARACTER EVOLUTION
Unleash Your Potential. Embrace Growth. Transform Your Journey.

Copyright © 2024 Adam Holbrook LLC

All rights reserved. No part of this book may be reproduced, distributed, or transmitted in any form or by any means, including photocopying, recording, or other electronic or mechanical methods, without the written permission from the publisher or author, except as permitted by US copyright law or in the case of brief quotations embodied in a book review.

Disclaimer: Although the publisher and the author have made every effort to ensure that the information in this book was correct at press time and while this publication is designed to provide accurate information in regard to the subject matter covered, the publisher and the author assume no responsibility for errors, inaccuracies, omissions, or any other inconsistencies herein and hereby disclaim any liability to any party for any loss, damage, or disruption caused by errors or omissions, whether such errors or omissions result from negligence, accident, or any other cause.

Interior Layout and Design by Stephanie Anderson
Book Cover Design by Abigael Elliott

ISBN:
979-8-89165-134-0 *Paperback*
979-8-89165-135-7 *Hardback*
979-8-89165-136-4 *E-book*

Published by:
Streamline Books
Kansas City, MO
streamlinebookspublishing.com

To my wife, Karen. Thank you for accepting me for who I am.
You inspire me to live my message even when it is difficult.

For my kids, Tenley and Trent. Thank you for
making life fun and being my guiding lights.

I love you all.

CONTENTS

INTRODUCTION

HAVE YOU EVER found yourself actively pursuing a goal, investing countless hours and energy, only to fall short despite consistent hard work and knowledge acquisition? I certainly have, and it led me to a crucial realization: working hard and gaining knowledge, while important, have their limitations. However, a well-developed character has been proven time and time again as the most valuable resource to overall success, fulfillment, and happiness.

I know this firsthand, as my personal journey has been marked by struggles with character flaws that caused my life to fall apart, ultimately leaving me suicidal. Faced with constant setbacks, I invested extensive hours in the self-examination, repair, and rebuilding of my character. The result was a transformative evolution that propelled my personal growth. Although I still make daily mistakes, I now recognize when my integrity is at stake and have the skills to mend errors, ensuring they no longer jeopardize my identity.

In this book, we'll go beyond traditional and often overly conceptual "advice" about growth and overcoming challenges, and you'll walk away with an actionable guide to inspire positive change.

Anyone can pretend to be someone on a good day, but how you act when life is against you defines your character. Character gives you the courage to keep your head up with pride and honor, something that knowledge and work ethic will not always provide. Character is taking ownership of your life, not blaming others for your failures. That's why I'm thrilled to bring you the ten character traits that will help you become more aware of who you are while taking you where you want to go. Each chapter focuses on one character trait; as you go through them, you'll discover what might be holding you back, along with strategies to move forward more effectively.

Each character trait we'll explore together in these chapters—gratitude, awareness, forgiveness, and more—includes steps structured as rungs on a ladder, adding clarity and direction when you feel especially lost and providing a path to ascend to inner fulfillment.

Each rung is actionable and designed to leave you with strategies you can apply and questions you can ask yourself to make your journey more linear.

I want you to know that this journey is personal to me. Though it has at times been hard-earned, as you'll see in this book, I've come to understand that developing our character is the key to a better life.

> In a world full of advice and opinions about what to do when you feel stuck, the answer is and always has been inside of us.

I hope *Character Evolution* leads you to a place where you feel more aware, accepted, and accomplished.

Let's get started.

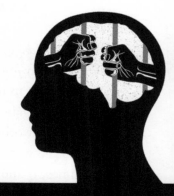

CHAPTER 1

BE GRATEFUL

Acquiring an attitude of gratitude will lead you where you want to go.

It is easy for him to be grateful and positive. Look at his life. He has everything. The perfect relationship, plenty of successful friends. He gets to do whatever he wants and has tons of money. He has no clue what it's like to struggle.

THAT WAS MY reaction when I was introduced to the notion of gratitude solving all of my problems by the keynote speaker at the business marketing seminar I was invited to attend. The speaker explained that changing my attitude to gratitude would change my life from lack to abundance. He even presented an exercise designed to teach us how to practice gratitude.

I thought to myself, *Don't waste my time with a foolish lesson to trick me into being grateful. That is complete and utter nonsense. How about giving me your successful career, perfect body, and health—then I will be grateful. Come live my life, and I will prove your nonsense statement of having, showing, and giving gratitude is the biggest crock of horse manure you have ever heard to solve all of my problems!*

At that point in my life, I had a victim mindset. I believed the world was against me. I believed the reason I wasn't getting ahead was that others were taking advantage of me. People would do me wrong, and in turn, I would do them wrong. Many times, if another person did me wrong, I would even take it out on multiple people who hadn't done a thing to me.

On top of that, I would yell, argue, belittle, and try to overpower anyone that didn't see it my way.

Sometimes the repercussions of doing another wrong wouldn't show up immediately, but karma always found its way back to me. My life was spiraling out of control.

I owned a commercial office cleaning business at the time and had worked around a hundred hours each week for almost three years. I employed around fourteen employees, depending on the day. I had a dream of becoming wealthy but was going about it all wrong, which caused me to get beat up day after day.

I remember I hired an employee to clean the floors and bathrooms at the YMCA campground in Stillwater, New Jersey. I initially liked him because he met my demands and treated me like the god I believed I was. I was even able to manipulate him into working overnight shifts he didn't want. Furthermore, he wanted to be paid ten dollars per hour, which was reasonable, but I knew I could get him to work for eight dollars per hour, as he needed the job.

After training him for three days, he asked me for a cash advance, which he claimed was to prevent his landlord from evicting him. I agreed to give him the thousand dollars and had him sign a loan contract.

The next day he didn't show up to work. This wasn't the first time I had gotten burned by an employee, but I was determined this would be the last. I decided I would show up at his apartment and get my money back.

Furious, I began pounding on his door while screaming. At first, it appeared he wasn't home, as there was no answer. But I wasn't giving up. After banging my fist some more, he finally opened the door.

"Give me my money back!" I yelled.

"I don't have it. I spent it," he responded.

I decided to plow into his apartment, looking around for something of value I could take. The apartment was bare, with only a mattress on the floor and some clothes scattered about.

Then I saw a window air conditioning unit. I went over to the window, put my arms around it, and yanked the unit out, ripping the screws that secured it out of the wall. I glared at him and said, "I'm taking this." I held the unit in a giant bear hug while walking out the apartment door, claiming a false victory.

The only *gratitude* I felt was to the universe for making the following day record-breaking heat so he would sweat his butt off.

Looking back, I'm able to realize my lack of compassion, lack of appreciation, and tendency to be controlling led to this situation unfolding.

A few weeks before this incident, I had visited my manager at one of the accounts he cleaned for me. Our relationship was good and revolved around work and sexualizing women. It was part of our regular routine to talk about my dates and other women as objects. When I showed up to check on him, he was drunk on the job. I found him slurring his speech, unable to stand. In his mumbled explanation, he told me his girlfriend threw him out of the apartment they shared because he had cheated on her, and he was now living on the streets.

I was frustrated with him but was afraid to fire him since I didn't have anyone to take over his shifts. It would take me months to find and train someone to do all of his accounts. I felt trapped. I decided to double down.

I bought an air mattress, a mini fridge fully stocked with food, and set up a bedroom for him in the extra office room where I rented space. My only rule was that he needed to be out of the building by 7:00 a.m. so other tenants or the land-lord wouldn't discover our secret and evict us. He lived at my office rent free for three months. In the end, we had a blowup, which caused the employment to end.

The only *gratitude* I felt was of self-restraint. For not tying him up, throwing him in my trunk, driving in the middle of the woods, and dropping him there to fight for his life with the wildlife.

As I reflect, I realize I wasn't a good role model. I could only imagine how my disrespectful attitude toward women may have influenced him to cheat—a decision I know he regretted.

Girlfriend problems were not new to me either. I had allowed my girlfriend to move in with me after only knowing her for a few weeks. Very quickly, my role as a boyfriend included breaking my bathroom door down to steal the knife away from her as she sliced her wrists.

Looking back, I realized I was using her as my little project to see if I could mold her into the perfect girlfriend in my eyes. But no matter what she did, it was never enough to meet my unrealistic expectations. That is why I believe she left me for another guy.

The only *gratitude* I had for her was learning firsthand all about suicide because, honestly, that had sounded like a pretty good idea to me as well.

Then it all came to a head on Christmas Eve 2005. I had a drink in one hand and my suicide note in the other. I had pictured it a million times: taking my car, driving off a cliff, and ending my life. I was drunk, numb, and ready.

My ungrateful, unappreciative victim attitude had caused my life to come crashing down.

My dad called me late that night to wish me a Merry Christmas and told me he loved me, which wasn't something he normally did. This caused me to cry myself to sleep in the car. I didn't realize it at the time, but I had only needed one more day. I was at rock bottom.

Rock bottom is a miraculous place. It is the place where you have no gratitude for anything or anyone. It is where life knocks you out cold, and you stop trying and stop pretending. It is a place where you don't care about your family, friends, financial situation, or life.

Then something happens. You begin to feel liberated, and you don't have anything to lose. You become free of everyone and everything. At that moment, you can breathe again, and it feels good. Nothing matters but your next breath.

At that moment, I decided to post my business for sale. Within four months, it had sold for $220,000; more money than I had ever seen in my twenty-seven years.

For the first time in my adult life, I was genuinely *grateful*. I was grateful for a new beginning.

A few months later, I had my first date with my future wife. This girl was different from anyone I had known. She was grateful and positive. That is why she claimed she was experiencing much success in her personal and professional life. She had an *attitude of gratitude.*

I remembered the advice given at that business seminar many years prior and knew that if I was going to keep this girl, I'd better give this gratitude thing a shot. I slowly started to fake my gratitude, which caused me to get some wins. This caused me to become more grateful, which caused me to have more wins. Soon gratitude overtook me, and with hard work, determination, and having an attitude of gratitude, I finally realized I could get anything I wanted in life. Does that mean I don't have any problems? No, I have just as many problems as most people. But when you have an attitude of gratitude, the good becomes better, and the bad isn't quite as bad as it once seemed. Having an attitude of gratitude can take you from where you are to where you want to go.

> *Having an attitude of gratitude*
> *can take you from where you are*
> *to where you want to go.*

Gratitude is the highest form of appreciation. It is the feeling and the sense of being completely satisfied with a situation, self, another person, or place.

Gratitude has no contingencies. You can't say you're grateful for something, and add a *but* at the end of the statement, like this:

- I love my wife, but I wish she would get a better job.
- I love my job, but I wish I got paid more.
- I love helping people, but I wish they would appreciate me more.

Only concentrate on the positive. There can be no negativity or ulterior motive within your words.

If the concept of gratitude for attaining everything you want in life is new to you, like it was to me in 2005, I understand. You may get annoyed with others when you hear about how grateful they are. You are probably jealous of others who have what you want. You probably pity yourself and have a victim's mindset. You might feel trapped and not know how to begin.

So let's start there. At the beginning.

THE GRATITUDE LADDER

That is why I developed the Gratitude Ladder: so you can ease your way into being grateful and experience more inner fulfillment, which in turn means more wins. As you climb the five rungs of the Gratitude Ladder, you will experience more joy, peace, and fulfillment.

First Rung: Force It

In the beginning, when life has you knocked down, you have to force gratitude. Force yourself into a feeling. I know it sounds ridiculous, but it works. Try it. Feel grateful for something or someone. Start with something small and straightforward. It could be anything (your health, food, a relationship, a job, a roof over your head, eyesight, etc.). Concentrate on the feeling of joy.

In the beginning, your list may have only a few items, but try expanding it as you gain additional awareness throughout your days.

It's always a good idea to review and update your gratitude list. As you do, you will notice how far you have come instead of concentrating on how far you have to go.

Another practice to adopt is a gratitude mantra. That means repeating everything that is going well for you. Say it out loud to yourself or others. Over and over. Our family takes turns going around our meal table or when on long car drives, saying what we are grateful for. The longer we play, the easier it is to overcome obstacles, face problems, or overcome difficult times. This forces us to feel good.

When you hear of others around you having success, make it a point to share in their excitement. Dive into their feelings and emotions. Be happy you have someone in your life getting wins because you are now on the same frequency as them, which means your time is coming.

Second Rung: Keep It

Stay with that feeling as long as possible. Fight the urge to let any negative thoughts in. Always think about the positive aspects of a person, place, thing, or idea. Keep that feeling. You get to control your mind. Your mind controls your words. Keep those thoughts positive. It will likely be more difficult than you think. The longer you can keep the "grateful" feeling, the easier it will be next time. In the beginning, you will find yourself fighting to keep those thoughts positive. If you slip into the negative, forgive yourself and tell yourself you will do better next time. It's only a matter of time before you can control your thoughts, and those thoughts control your future.

Third Rung: Believe It

Concentrate your thoughts on believing and owning that gratitude. Convince yourself that you are now a new person and you are going to live your life confidently and full of so much energy your gratitude will be contagious. Continue to repeat this over and over until you're fully immersed in joy. The universe is waiting on you and will deliver once you believe.

Believing your life will change is hard work. That little low-self-worth devil appears on your shoulder time and time again, trying to push away your gains. "Go back to your old self. Your life isn't going to change. You're not as good as others," he whispers. Get a hold of yourself and know, when you commit to believing, you will be receiving.

That devil has appeared on my shoulder quite a few times and still tries coming back. When I started each of my three businesses, he made appearances. "You're not going to be successful. Give up and work for someone else," he declared. Each time he made an appearance, I began to compare myself and became jealous. Each time I choose an emotion other than gratitude, I choose to limit my potential.

Fourth Rung: Show It

Give compliments and tell others what you are grateful for. Start pushing yourself to speak more positively. When asked, "How are you doing," answer "I'm doing great," or "Awesome," instead of the boring "I'm good," or "Fine." Speak about what is wonderful in your life instead of your struggles.

Show your gratitude by giving a hug, making a thank-you card, giving a compliment, or sending a text message to express your appreciation. I love to give a compliment each time I'm with someone because it shows them how much I care.

After a while, you will be able to control the outcome of your life with gratitude, and you will be able to play with it as if it were a game. Life doesn't need to be hard. It can be everything you want it to be.

True gratitude is unconditional and doesn't depend on specific circumstances or outcomes. It is the appreciation for what is, without expecting something in return.

Many people live in what-ifs, speaking of when they win the lottery or when their health and relationships will improve. They also relive old times, talking about "the good old days" or when they scored four touchdowns in a single game. I get that. I love dreaming and envisioning the future because it guides me to where I want to go, and I also love bringing up stories of the past with my buddies because it connects me to old friends.

But the truth is that dreaming and reliving takes us out of the present moment and into the future or back to the past. If you are consistently looking to the future or looking to the past, you are failing to be in the present, which delays your happiness. Happiness is experienced in the present and influenced by our mindsets. While memories of the past and excitement of the future can contribute to overall well-being, the ability to feel true happiness lies in how we approach and appreciate the current moment. Be happy now. Be happy with what you have while working on what you want.

The more gratitude you have now, the more beautiful surprises life has in store for you later.

Tipping point: Once you reach a point where your positive thoughts and words outweigh the negative thoughts and words, your world will shift. The positive thoughts begin to multiply, causing everything around you to change.

Fifth Rung: Climb It

From what I've observed in many grateful individuals, there's a clear link between the most fulfilled and successful people and what they appreciate the most. As you review the tiers of gratitude below, ask yourself where most of your gratitude lies and how you can ascend tiers in the future.

Lower Tier: Gratitude for Physical Items

If you fall into this group, odds are you're very confident and determined. You probably have lots of friends because you are usually more concerned with what you look like on the outside than on the inside. There isn't anything wrong with that, because it brings awareness to grow yourself on the inside to match your external actions. To become better on the inside, we must first determine what we value from our outside actions. You begin to build credibility with yourself, which eventually will allow what you look like on the outside to catch up with what you are on the inside. Examples of gratitude for physical items include focusing on things like your car, money, a nice bottle of wine, designer clothing, or great seats to a sporting event.

If most of your gratitude is for physical items, it eventually leads to feeling lost and needing more self-purpose. You will find yourself living for the future instead of being in the present.

This will result in always chasing more physical items and never being content with what you have.

Physical items are a great place to kick-start you into being grateful, but they are only a pit stop as you align who you are attempting to be on the outside with who you actually are.

Middle Tier: Gratitude for Existing

If you're in this group, odds are you have a pretty good life balance. You also likely recognize your physical and emotional needs and have impeccable awareness of what changes you need to make. Well done. People who consistently have gratitude for existing are content with life and live in the present moment. Examples of gratitude for existing include focusing on things like breath, mindset, and awareness.

But still, I know you want more out of life. You are questioning your purpose. You want to make a bigger impact in this world and live with intention. You want to change the world. That is why you aren't going to stop at the middle tier.

Higher Tier: Gratitude for Others

If you're in this group, odds are that you appreciate and acknowledge the kindness, support, or positive impact you have on the lives of others—and that others have in your life. It involves recognizing your contributions and expressing thanks for others' presence, actions, or assistance. You believe giving is the key to everything in life, and you know the key to giving is caring for others. You lead by example. Examples of gratitude for others may include focusing on the following:

- being grateful for a teacher or mentor who has helped you
- being grateful for a financial advisor to balance your portfolio
- being grateful for your misbehaving kids who taught you how to maintain self-control
- being grateful to your partner who cooks dinner for your family

You wouldn't be where you are in life if it wasn't for others. Consistently showing your appreciation will help you go from struggling to thriving.

WHAT'S NEXT?

Most people fail to allow gratitude to change their life because they don't buy into it. They lack self-worth and define themselves as others define them. They are so busy trying to be something they are not that they fail to become who they are and fail to realize what they are capable of being. By living in this cycle, they are insecure, jealous, and frustrated. They are dependent on others instead of finding freedom to become who they are.

If you claim to be grateful, you must be content with what you have and where you are. Release yourself from needing anything you don't possess. As you grow, remember to always check in with yourself and remind yourself to have an attitude of gratitude.

Ready to practice gratitude for yourself? Try these two strategies:

Make a List

What do you feel gratitude for? On a blank piece of paper, make a list of at least twenty specific items you are grateful for and why. Here are some examples:

1. *My wife*: She is a great mom, she lets me be me, and she helps to provide for our family.
2. *My house*: It keeps me warm, safe, and comfortable.
3. *My exercise routine*: It keeps me balanced, healthy, and in good shape.
4. *My kids*: They give me a sense of purpose, and I can empower them while improving myself.
5. *My pet*: My dog loves me unconditionally, gets me out of the house to exercise, and keeps me safe.

Play the Gratitude Game

Each time you comment negatively or judge a person, place, or thing, put a dollar in a designated jar. You can play with the entire family or just a friend—the point is that you just start. This activity forces you to feel your emotions and actively switch your gratitude meter on high. Soon, you will have enough money in the jar to celebrate your new self.

CHAPTER 2

BE SELF-AWARE

*Every frustration is an opportunity
to get to know yourself better.*

Doing dishes is a waste of my time.

THAT'S WHAT I thought each morning and evening as I looked at the sink, overflowing with dishes. My perspective was that taking care of the mess would hinder me from being productive in what would *actually* help me succeed.

I'd often think about using paper plates, so I didn't need to face the battle of doing dishes. I'd tried to con my kids into doing the dishes, sure. But after the excitement of the first day wore off, they gave up, and I was back at it. I even had a conversation with my wife about hiring someone to do them for us.

I was so consumed with being miserable and frustrated that I was failing to look inside myself to gain the awareness I needed to find any solutions. I just wanted the entire family to know I hated doing the dishes.

Well, that is what I initially thought.

I decided I needed to find another way. I started searching for solutions within myself. I needed to become aware of the true reason I hated doing the dishes.

As I began to gain clarity, I realized it wasn't the task of doing dishes I hated, but rather losing the time it took. I wanted more time for something I loved: reading. The dishes were getting in the way of my reading time, so I needed to figure out a solution.

That is when I had an *aha* moment and figured out what to do.

Immediately after doing the dishes, I take Luna, our dog, on a short walk. I decided I would listen to audiobooks while walking Luna and extend my walks longer. This has also led me to bring my audiobooks on car rides. I was used to playing music in the car or making a call to pass the time. My new routine has been truly amazing. I now look forward to doing dishes because I know, after they are done, I get to listen to my audiobook, and Luna ends up with a much longer walk.

Our frustrations are due to the lack of awareness of the changes we need to make within ourselves. If you had more awareness in your life, you wouldn't be taking your stress out on your partner, coworkers, family, or dishes. It's not their fault you choose to make or not make decisions that have brought you to this point in your life. Most people blame their situations on an outside source. Whether it's another person, the environment, the situation, or luck. They are waiting around wishing for something to change. But wishing isn't a strategy. Those who search outside themselves wish. Those who search within themselves awaken. Achieving more fulfillment and happiness can be found in altering your thought process, and it all starts with cultivating awareness.

> *Those who search outside*
> *themselves wish.*
> *Those who search within*
> *themselves awaken.*

To gain internal peace, spend time with yourself and gain the awareness you need to kick start your future self. When examining your life and what may need changing, begin by playing with different possibilities in your mind. We often believe we must know all the answers before beginning a new routine. This isn't true. All we need to know is what needs to be changed. All change begins with awareness. Do you think I knew how to manage employees when I had my first business? Nope. Do you think I knew how to write this book when I started? Nope. Do you think I knew how to transform my body to get on stage in a men's bodybuilding contest? Not at all. But as I began, I gained the awareness of what I needed to do next. I don't get frustrated nearly as often as I did before. When I gain the awareness of my frustrations, I take control of myself. If something needs to be changed, I start by making the smallest alteration to my routine and see how it feels. This propels me to what the next small modification is. I play with it in my mind as I commit to change. This will ultimately get me from where I am to where I want to go.

People often believe their frustrations stem from others or circumstances out of their control. But that simply is not true. Stop blaming others for everything that is wrong in your life. Real change begins inside of you. Every frustration is an opportunity to get to know yourself better. Pause, breathe, and ask yourself, "Why am I upset?" Dive into your awareness and explore the real reason why something is frustrating you. Get a hold of your life and take ownership of it; become aware of the changes you must make.

Below are examples of various frustrations, including who the person directs their frustration toward, the genuine cause of the frustration, and a proactive solution. In every case, it's essential to recognize that *you*—not any external factor—are responsible for the frustration. Taking control of your life involves gaining awareness, finding a pathway forward, and taking action.

FRUSTRATION	PERSON YOU'RE TAKING FRUSTRATION OUT ON	REAL REASON FOR FRUSTRATION	SOLUTION/ AWARENESS
Your spouse cooks too much food	Spouse	You gained weight	Self-control or exercise
Your parents try to control you	Parents	You just want to live your own life	Limit interactions/ create boundaries
There isn't enough time	Everyone around you	Lack of planning	Create an online calendar

In all cases, it is about gaining awareness within yourself and not blaming something or someone else for your frustration. After achieving awareness, commit to an action plan. It's essential to note that no plan is worth the paper it's written on if it doesn't lead to taking action.

Today is a good day to begin. How about right now? Stop making promises to yourself and others you won't keep. Failing to follow through quickly erodes your character, making it difficult for yourself and others to take you seriously. Break free from this cycle to avoid sabotaging your life further. As you commit and gain control of yourself, your life will change.

Stop looking for external factors to change for you to live the life you want. Stop wishing your partner would change. Stop wishing you had a better job, better health, more time, better friends, or more money. Diving into your awareness provides clarity, guiding you toward a better situation and further enjoyment.

Climb the rungs of the Awareness Ladder.

THE AWARENESS LADDER

> *"To grow yourself, you must know yourself."*
> —JOHN MAXWELL

To reach your potential, you must build on what you learned in the past. To do that, you must realize who you are and where you want to go.

What are you currently caught up in? Climb the Awareness Ladder, turn your frustrations into successes, and gain more fulfillment.

First Rung: Make a List

Dive into your awareness like never before. You have the power to change your trajectory by examining your life. What is currently frustrating you or something you want to change? Is it your body weight? Is it your career? Is it your business, your health, or your relationship? Is it doing dishes? Is it your friends or family? You can never achieve a better life unless you become focused on what you want. To do this, you must examine your life.

> *"An unexamined life is not worth living."*
> —SOCRATES

Stop, reflect, and examine.

Create a list of your current frustrations. Think about the following areas of your life: financial, career, business, fun time, health and fitness, relationships, and serving and giving to others. What specifically would you like to change in each area? List at least one item or situation in each area.

Second Rung: Be Specific

Real change develops by diving into the specifics of what you want to change. This opens your mind by searching within yourself. Dive into your emotions about the situation. What are those feelings? Make them about you and your frustrations. They are never contingent on what others did or what others should do.

Gain awareness of the specifics you would like to change. It isn't about the external factors we can't control, but about *you*.

We are often so dependent on others for our own happiness that we fail to look inside ourselves for the answers.

This rung brings struggles and causes people to get hung up because most want to point the finger at an outside source as the reason they are feeling frustrated. They would rather remain frustrated at another and make their fulfillment contingent upon what another does instead of being the change they seek. Such as:

- I will show the love my partner craves when she does her fair share of the housework.
- I would be in a good mood if that car hadn't cut me off.
- Once my boss gives me that promotion, I will be happy.
- I will feel better once my friends stop bragging about all the money they make.

This rung is about diving into the actual frustrations and becoming aware of what needs to change. Here are some examples:

Example 1

- **Frustration:** My family counts on me to give them money.
- **What I want to change:** I no longer want to give them money.

Do not go into a long rationale to support your feelings. Do not fall into fear by thinking if you stop giving them money, they will disown you. Each time you go down this side road, you slip into the victim and will never be on a worthwhile course. Keep your focus on the frustration and what you want to change. Done.

Example 2

- **Frustration:** Your friend doesn't call you back.
- **What I want to change:** I want to have people in my life that return my calls. This isn't about changing your friend. This is about you and the changes you can make.

Example 3

- **Frustration:** I hate my job.
- **What I want to change:** I want to get out of a cubicle.

Now that you have the awareness of what is really hindering you from reaching your potential, you can move on to the third rung.

Third Rung: Envision Possibility

Do you know exactly what would bring you happiness and lasting fulfillment? I want you to describe what the ideal situation would look like. Could you do it? Forget about what was, what has been, or what it is currently. I want you to open your mind to the possibility of having that ideal situation. Why do you want this? What would it look like, and how would you feel when you have it?

I want you to imagine and let your mind play with all the possibilities. How would you feel, act, move, and talk if you had it now?

What would be your ideal friendship, your ideal body, your ideal mate, and your ideal lifestyle?

I have two giant whiteboards (my vision board) hanging in my home office that give me clarity when I get stuck. This reinforces my path when life gets messy.

One whiteboard is my long-term vision board, and the other is my one-year plan. I break down my visions into categories (Financial, Career, Fun Time, Health and Fitness, Relationships, and Serving and Giving to Others). Under each category I write what my vision is and what I'm working towards in each of those categories. The purpose is to visualize what I want and remind myself of the direction I must work toward each day.

This keeps me focused on the present moment and today.

Fourth Rung: Assess Your Skills

Does your ability match your desires?

In high school, I wanted to be a professional golfer. I played on the golf team and was always pretty good. I had some natural talent and worked extremely hard to develop my skills. I played all the time and even had lessons to fine-tune my game. I dreamed of the day I would be on TV making that winning putt to beat John Daly in the US Open. The problem was I wasn't being honest with myself. With as much talent as I had, and as hard as I worked, I could never reach that elite status. My swing speed wasn't quick enough, and my talent wasn't good enough to play on tour. I knew that, but I wasn't being honest with myself. I wanted to live in a dream world.

Do your wants in life match your skill set? What areas are you gifted in? We all have certain areas where we excel. Spending time developing our strengths will allow us to thrive and develop a successful road map into the future. Many focus on addressing their weaknesses. They think this will help them in life. But if you improve at a weakness, the best you can become is average, and average won't make you reach your potential. Find areas you enjoy and are gifted in and spend time developing them to become not just good, but great.

Fifth Rung: Uncover Your *Why*

What is the real reason you want to do what you want to do? Is it money or fame? Is it to boss people around? What is your *why?* Doing something for status will never give you consistent strength long term. A *why* is clear, concise, includes your core values, main priorities, and what you are working towards. It narrows your focus and allows you to spend time and energy where it matters most.

Your *why* is what guides you and keeps you on track to move in the direction you want. Is your *why* strong enough that you will keep going and keep getting up when life gets tough?

You will fail tons of times while moving towards your vision. If your *why* isn't strong enough, you will quit. Anything worthwhile in life takes work.

Creating a *why* is never based on money or gaining power. If your *why's* main objective is attached to status or accumulation, you will always be chasing more and never working toward something real. Once you make a million, you will want three million. If you have two houses, you will want three. Once you have fifteen stores, you will want twenty. You delay your happiness and fulfillment until a later time.

Here are some examples of *why* statements that may point you in the right direction.

- I want to energize and empower school leaders to have a successful classroom. (This is one of my *whys*.)
- I want to live a life of significance by helping my team reach their potential.
- I want to inspire children to be more than they thought possible.
- I want to use my writing skills to inspire and educate others around the world to make changes.

Sixth Rung: Chart Your Course

Many times we get overwhelmed by the task at hand. We don't know what to do first, second, or third. We may not even know what we need to do. Make a list. Write down as many changes as you can think of that will move you in your new desired direction.

It doesn't matter if your list is long or only has a few items. As you move further along the path, the light will become brighter, and the next moves will become clearer. The most fulfilled, successful people in the world don't have all the answers and don't know exactly where to begin. They aren't afraid of failure—they welcome it. They are excited to fail so they can learn what didn't work and do it better next time. Prioritizing your list is a great way to get started. But don't consume too much energy determining what could come first, next, or last. It's most important that you have a path forward. You must constantly adjust, adapt, and change directions as you move along on your journey.

For example, if your *why* statement is to lose weight and become healthier so you can have more energy to play with your children, the task may sound overwhelming. But having a list of changes you could make breaks down the task into manageable steps. Below are some ideas you may consider to start you on this journey.

- Fasting: Eat all my meals in an eight-hour period, noon to 8:00 p.m.
- Walk for thirty minutes during lunch.
- Buy a sixty-four-ounce reusable water bottle and drink one bottle per day.
- Track my calories on an app.
- Go to the gym two times per week for forty-five minutes.
- Replace my snacks with a cup of tea.
- Instead of going out for dinner once a week, go out for a movie with no snacks.
- Buy new gym equipment.

Looking at the above list could be overwhelming. Which one thing could you start with?

The point of the list isn't to start doing everything at once; it is to uncover areas that could open the door to the next move. Breaking the task into manageable changes to build on.

Start by choosing one new activity. See how your body responds. After a few weeks, adjust and add another. Before you know it, you will incorporate all the changes, discover new ones, modify old ones, and keep building from what you started with. Soon you will lose weight and become healthier and set your limits even higher.

Seventh Rung: Applying and Evaluating

Now that the plan is in place, take action.

Stop talking about what you're going to accomplish. Do it. Are you a sayer or a doer? You don't need to let others know what you intend to do.

Deciding and doing are not the same. So many talented people don't reach their potentials because they don't take action. A good idea without action is like a house without walls. If you want to lose weight, become a better partner, get a better job, or improve your circumstances, you have to do something about it.

Everything worthwhile in life takes work.

In working toward your greatest accomplishments, there will be a period of time when nothing happens. You are trying and failing and trying and failing. You learn, you adjust, and you fail some more. You want to give up; you want to quit. That is why 70 percent of new businesses fail within two to five years and approximately 40 to 50 percent of first marriages end in divorce. That is why 95 percent of diets fail and most dieters return to their starting weight within two years. Everything of value in life takes work.

When you begin something new and make changes, there is a period of time when most of your progress is under the ground. You can't see it, which is why you are so burned out and frustrated and want to stop doing it. You may gain self-doubt and lose self-confidence.

You probably won't see any results from exercise until months after you begin.

You won't be making much money after a few years of working hundreds of hours building a business. The results are there, but they are hidden. To uncover the results, you must consistently put in the work, day after day.

We live in a country where we want immediate results and instant gratification. We have get-slim quick-diets and get-rich-quick-businesses. Sure, you may get some results with these schemes. However, they never last. If you want lasting results, you have to put the work in consistently over a long period of time. You cannot think about it in terms of arriving at the results you want, but instead diligently working day in and day out with no end date. It is a continuous journey. If you want something bad enough, you will put the work in, gain additional knowledge, and consistently design your schedule around the habits that will move you there.

One strategy that has worked well for me is having an accountability partner. My partner is my buddy, Dr. Brett Caminez. Every Tuesday at 11:00 a.m., we jump on a phone call to talk about what we accomplished during the past week, reflecting on what could be improved and what we want to accomplish in the upcoming week. We support each other, aren't jealous, and possess positive attitudes. Whenever I get stuck, I know he can help me through it. Working with him for several years has magnified my growth, and I believe it has done the same for him. I'm incredibly grateful for our friendship.

Do you have someone who can keep you on track? If you don't, I want to encourage you to keep making yourself better. As you do, other growing people will find their way to you.

Are you fighting to reach a destination—whether it is a promotion, a healthy body weight, or a certain lifestyle? Some people put the hard work in consistently, and when they arrive, they think they can stop. I've seen this happen time and time again. The destination may feel good initially because it is directly tied to their egos, but the ego fades quickly, and the journey continues.

If you are always jumping companies, diet plans, workout plans, or business ideas, you will always be chasing and never achieving. The longer you work toward something, the more consistent you are, and the more you evaluate and apply your newfound knowledge, the greater your success and fulfillment will be. Jumping around will burn you out and keep you stuck in mediocrity.

Are you repeating the same thing and expecting a different result?

That is the formula for disaster. If your weight loss has capped, your business isn't growing, and your relationships are failing, you need to adjust. You have made great strides to get to this point, but to grow more, you need to steer in another direction. Just because it worked in the past doesn't mean it will work again. Taking action is only half of the formula. Constantly evaluating and applying what you learned will propel you forward.

Wouldn't it be fun to see how far you can go in life? Play with it, reflect on what is working and what isn't, and adjust.

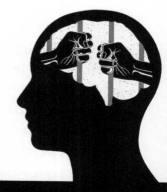

CHAPTER 3

BE FORGIVING

Forgiveness is never about the other; it's about you.

You're messing with the wrong person. If you do me wrong, I will always get my sweet revenge. I will never forget what you did, and I promise to bring you down even if I have to go down with you.

THAT USED TO be my attitude when someone took advantage of me, argued politics, gave unsolicited advice, cut me off on the highway, or disagreed with me.

I was holding onto so much hurt that I didn't have many close friends, and the side effects led to my downfall.

When I screwed up, I would never admit it or apologize. I would turn the tables, twisting the plot or belittling the person for what they had done at another point, which I falsely justified as the reason for my outburst.

I would never forgive myself or others, which caused me to pile up all this hate, anger, and frustration. My world was consumed with people who did me wrong, and in turn, I did them wrong. My life was so unbearable that I started to lash out at people who never hurt me.

If a girl cheated on me, I would find another girl and cheat on her. If an employee would steal from me, I would purposely forget to run payroll for the entire company. If you forced yourself into my driving lane to make a turn, I would deliberately try to drive you off the road.

I would manipulate you to apologize, and it needed to live up to my acceptable standards. If it didn't, I would correct you and make you apologize exactly how I saw fit.

I never fully forgave others or myself; I let grievances pile up on my score sheet, accumulating on the sidelines, waiting to throw them into the fire and at their faces.

As you can probably imagine, holding these grudges limited my success, inner peace, and fulfillment.

Has or is someone physically or mentally hurting you or someone you deeply care about? Whether intentional or unintentional, it doesn't dismiss the pain you are facing or have faced. An outside source has come into your life and flipped your world upside down.

Releasing the pain from the hurt you are experiencing is no doubt the hardest thing in the world to do. You might feel angry, trapped, scared, frustrated, and physically want to get revenge on the person.

Depending on the severity of the circumstances and your coping skills, you may have trouble getting through a day, an hour, or a minute without feeling trapped. You shut down, your insides are in constant pain, and you don't allow others into your world. Others may dismiss your feelings because they are sick of hearing about them.

You might even feel smothered in your skin and that the walls are closing in on you. Your breathing, well-being, stress levels, personality, and other relationships are all affected.

You search within yourself time and time again, hoping the deep hurt will go away, but just like a reliable clock, the pain stays deep in your gut.

Others will try to advise and tell you to snap out of it. You have forgotten who you are or who you were, and you want nothing to do with anyone in your life. You have no idea where or how to start over. Your thoughts slip to picking up and leaving everyone who loves you and moving across the country where nobody knows your name. Somewhere you can start over and mask your identity.

But you continue to allow the daily dose of torture because you feel like you deserve it.

I understand if you have been down that road or are currently there. It is a dark place where some can sit for years. I have been there a few times, and this is exactly how I felt.

You want to become better and not have to feel this pain again. You know it's time to forgive and let go of the emotions holding you back from a better future, but you don't know how to begin.

When you are genuinely ready to begin the healing process, forgiving the person who hurt you will free you and give you the mental health to heal yourself. So many times, we allow someone else's actions to affect us negatively. You don't want to give in because you know that person will continue to hurt you again and again. You need to teach them a lesson, but in the process, the pain is attacking you and may even make you sick. You try to carry on with life, but the feelings resurface. They may even be masked as anger for someone who didn't do anything to you. It's time to forgive. Don't forgive for their sake; do it for yourself.

Often, others don't want to forgive because they believe it shows a sign of weakness and gives permission for that person to hurt you even more. Checking in with yourself and creating safe boundaries after you forgive will allow you to move on with your life.

You may say what they did doesn't bother you. That is a big lie, and I guarantee it affects you. If you're talking about it, it bothers you. If you claim you have moved on, but still have negative words about the person when their name comes up, it still has a negative place inside of you.

Coming to a place where you realize you don't have the power to change another person is highly satisfying. They don't see it your way. As much as it is clear as day to you, it's not your job to tell others what to do or see. You become trapped in your own mind if you continue down this road. Furthermore, if you want the other person to suffer because they hurt you, you will drag yourself down with that ship.

> *If you want the other person to suffer because they hurt you, you will drag yourself down with that ship.*

It doesn't matter if you are forgiving someone who physically harmed you or emotionally scarred you. Coming to a place of forgiveness allows you to release your pain. Forgiving someone is never about the person who has hurt you. It is about you. You forgive someone so you can carry on with your life and not hide anymore. You can walk down the streets again, free, not needing to explain yourself to anyone, accepting the circumstances as they are while growing into what you want.

Just because you forgive someone doesn't mean you must go back to them, hang out with them, or see them often. By forgiving, you gain control back. Be careful about future relationship choices and reflect on your needs and boundaries to avoid this difficult situation again.

You may need professional help understanding your emotions so you can forgive yourself and others.

Above all, the healing process is about finding a way forward. If you aren't taking action, you are simply avoiding and delaying the recovery. Healing is about acting and finding a way forward, as simple or as difficult as that may sound.

Climb the rungs of the Forgiveness Ladder.

THE FORGIVENESS LADDER

First Rung: Accepting That the Pain Is Still There

Part of the recovery is processing the pain. You may feel angry, sad, scared, or have self-pity. You may be holding in your pain. Shutting down and not allowing yourself to process your feelings will prolong your recovery and could have a lot of adverse side effects. Each moment you choose to hold onto negative emotion is a moment of happiness lost. Forgiving someone doesn't mean condoning their behavior. Forgiveness is allowing negative feelings of outrage and grief to come in, and then letting them go because you want peace with your life.

I spent my entire childhood and most of my adult life holding grudges and not forgiving. I didn't know any different. It was how others were around me, and I thought it was completely normal. Everyone I spent time with talked about how hard and unfair life was. When I finally broke out of my bubble, I realized that life didn't need constant drama and hurt. I saw that it was possible to live in peace.

I hope you can find peace if you are reading this and struggling in your life. Trust me: the grass is greener on the other side.

Delaying Your Emotions

Whenever someone didn't respond the way I wanted, I would snap and try to overpower them by talking over them. This always led to an argument, which always led to someone apologizing, which always led to someone forgiving. Sometimes, I held grudges for days, weeks, or even years. It was a daily occurrence I hated but was secretly addicted to.

Then I was introduced to the idea of "delaying your emotions" by someone I respect and care deeply about. He said the key to a successful fulfilled life is not allowing your emotions to get the best of you. Delaying your emotions allows you to process what another is saying and realize there is never a positive outcome reacting without thinking. Nobody wants to deal with a hothead because it will limit how far you can go and affect your well-being. The longer you can delay your emotions when someone frustrates you, the easier the next time will be. If you do screw up, come clean and apologize. This will enable you to control the outcome of the situation. The next time someone frustrates you, stop, count to ten, take a deep breath, and process. You and your future self will be glad you did.

Did your kids do something they weren't supposed to? Did your parents say something that got under your skin? Did your spouse talk badly about you with one of your friends? Did your employee not show up for the meeting? Did your friend lie to you? Each time you respond and react negatively to others with anger or sadness you continue down the same, inevitably miserable, dead-end path.

At this point in my life, I have a positive attitude. It's not that I don't have problems or ever get frustrated. I do. I have the same amount of problems as most people, but I don't allow them to run my life. By delaying my emotions, I take control of my destiny.

Being Honest with Yourself

You may not have been able to control the events that have led to your suffering, but you have the power to release the negative emotions they caused.

Here are some questions to ask yourself to see whether you still hold onto emotional pain.

Is your health deteriorating? We often believe we have found a place and buried this emotional suffering. But it comes masked many times through your health deteriorating. In a WebMD article by R. Morgan Griffin titled "The 10 Problems Caused By Stress," they list heart disease, asthma, obesity, diabetes, headaches, depression, gastrointestinal problems, aging, and premature death as side effects of not dealing with stress. I could add many additional ailments to the list. If you are having health concerns, they could be tied to not processing your stress.

Are you avoiding going places, answering messages, or seeing people because you don't want confrontation? Do you believe hiding gives you the best chance at not having to beat your head against the wall and go through a continuous no-control circle of your life? Hiding from pain wears you down and crumples you up inside.

If you continually assert that you've moved on from a situation and it no longer affects you, it could be a distinct indication of inner distress. Discussing the situation suggests you still care, as true indifference would mean not discussing it at all. You are holding onto something that requires processing.

Second Rung: Releasing the Blame

You may say, *I didn't do anything. It's not my fault. I will feel better when that person understands what they did and apologizes in the way I believe they should.* If this is your response, you are holding onto your pride and unaware that you can improve. Too often, we have expectations of others that won't ever be filled. What they did was messed up, toxic, emotional, or physical, but that can't be your focus. Don't make excuses for another's behavior; make the situation right for you.

If you are angry or hurt, you haven't processed your emotions enough to move toward recovery. Others may even have a difference of opinion about what they did. Why do you care so much that they understand your side? Does it really matter if they don't see things the way you do? Curb your pride and the need to feed your fragile ego. Once you do, you can release the blame and become selfish toward your recovery.

Third Rung: Forgiving

Forgiveness is a powerful act of liberation, freeing oneself from the burden of resentment and pain. It is the acceptance that you are going to leave this situation and not allow additional internal or external forces to make you relapse. You are done, have forgiven, and want to move on.

Forgiving is not saying "I'm sorry," and still holding a grudge or gossiping about the situation. By accepting the situation, learning a lesson, and moving on, you become better.

Many times in the past, I have said I accepted another's apology yet still held that grudge, avoided that person, and spoke negatively about that situation. But forgiving is releasing the pain and moving on. You have had time to process; now it's about improving you.

Releasing negativity is critical to manifesting a better life; holding onto anger only builds obstacles on the path to a brighter future. Letting go of grievances allows room for positivity and personal growth.

Once you take that step, you'll experience a sense of relief— it's time, and you deserve it.

To initiate change, I had to begin by forgiving myself. I've made numerous mistakes that brought me to this point, and the crucial first step was self-forgiveness. Despite still making daily mistakes, I find liberation in forgiving myself. It's a profound emotional release—I'm letting go. By prioritizing self-forgiveness, I've cleansed my inner self, and it's a gratifying sensation. Throughout this process, I reflect on what I could have done differently, learning and adjusting for the future.

Stop Requiring an Apology

Release the need for an apology; forgiveness doesn't hinge on receiving one. Recognize that their perspective may differ from yours. Shift from seeking recognition to deepening understanding and cultivating compassion. Certain individuals may not possess the awareness or personal growth to acknowledge their mistakes and offer a sincere apology.

I like to apologize when I know I made a mistake; it helps humble my ego while building trust.

Fourth Rung: Determining Boundaries

After forgiving another, you may be vulnerable to a relapse. You have come a long way. Be proud of yourself. Now is the moment to discover a balance that suits you. Reflect on what you require to maintain peace and identify your needs. Don't blame others for your feelings; instead, be mindful of them. Resist external pressures trying to push you into actions you're uncomfortable with. Regularly check in with yourself and establish healthy boundaries to safeguard your well-being.

Boundaries must be adjusted, committed to, and tracked while gauging your overall wellness.

While discovering safe boundaries, consider:

Limiting Time Interaction

Instead of spending the entire day with the person you are recovering from, hang out with them for an hour. Let them know you have other plans and need to leave shortly. Instead of seeing this person every weekend, go once a month. Instead of calling every day, call one time per week. What has worked well for me is calling while driving in the car. When I arrive at my destination, getting off the phone is easy.

If someone doesn't like your boundaries and tries to guilt you, don't let them. This is about you. Stop being a people pleaser. Saying no can lead to reduced stress, clearer priorities, and the preservation of personal boundaries.

Protect Your Partner

Above all, in a relationship, prioritize boundaries that safeguard both you and your partner. Your partner's needs are always a priority as that person is your teammate. Avoid harming your relationship by speaking negatively about your partner; keep arguments private between the two of you. Always prioritize your partner over your children, parents, and friends, maintaining a strong foundation. When the relationship faces challenges, addressing them directly, rather than pretending everything is fine, is crucial.

Physical Safety and Boundaries

Although I am not qualified to offer professional advice on surviving abuse, I would like to share the story of how I was able to pull myself away from an abusive relationship. Getting out of an abusive relationship is not easy as there are a lot of factors that go into them. What worked for me may not work for you. If you are in an abusive relationship I recommend contacting the National Domestic Violence Helpline at 1-800-799-7233.

If you ever fear for your physical safety, it's crucial to remove this person from your life promptly. This is your most potent tool; staying in an abusive relationship erodes your sense of self, making it challenging to fulfill your life purpose. Waiting only intensifies the difficulty of severing ties completely. Leaving is painful and difficult but is vital for your well-being.

For some time, I was in an abusive relationship. In the beginning, I wanted out. I had never experienced physical abuse before. The more time went on, the more I thought I could change her, but instead, it made me addicted to the drama and unknown. Being in an unstable relationship was the most exhilarating thing I had in my life.

I remember getting punched in the face while driving on the highway, causing my eye to bleed. I pulled over to the side of the road in an attempt to kick her out of my car, only for her to instantly seduce me.

If only the relationship highs could be constant, it would have been the best. The thrill of the lows contributed to the greatness of the highs, but unfortunately, the lows consistently outlasted the highs.

Finally, I got enough courage and strength to end the relationship, a decision fraught with difficulty. The idea of returning crossed my mind repeatedly, and each day was consumed by pain. Although the prospect of returning to her was daunting, being alone was even scarier. I'm grateful for finding the strength to move forward, having forgiven her. I genuinely wish her peace and happiness.

If you find yourself on this path, I want to share the advice I gave myself: in a relationship where your physical safety is compromised, you need to get out before you become trapped. It will never be right. Get out now. The longer you wait, the more challenging it becomes to break free, and the more likely you'll keep returning. Take it one day at a time. One minute at a time. Do something that brings some satisfaction to get your mind off of it. Find positive, supportive people to be around. Once you commit to leaving, keep yourself busy and have a dedicated friend to support the transition.

As you grow, your ability to break down personal boundaries increases. The individuals who once frustrated you no longer hold that power, and as you become stronger, you will need fewer boundaries. Your world undergoes a transformation, influencing the people around you, enhancing your tolerance, and reshaping your interactions. Your growth allows you to connect with anyone, even those with opposing views. As you evolve, the universe aligns your relationships with those on a similar growth path.

Fifth Rung: Wish Happiness and Peace to Those Who Have Hurt You

At this juncture, you no longer harbor ill intentions for this individual. True forgiveness entails genuinely wishing them happiness and peace, channeling positive energy that, in turn, contributes to your own joy and serenity. This marks the essence of true forgiveness—you're healed, no longer relying on boundaries to safeguard your well-being. Your strength prevails, victorious in the battle of forgiveness.

In the journey of self-discovery and interpersonal growth, the ability to forgive oneself and others serves as a profound liberation. It's a transformative act that unshackles us from the weight of past mistakes and grievances, creating space for healing and personal evolution. It is a powerful choice that empowers us to move forward with resilience, grace, and a newfound sense of inner peace.

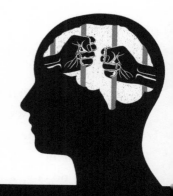

CHAPTER 4

BE EMPATHETICALLY UNDERSTANDING

Putting yourself in another's shoes.

I can't believe they called the cops on me.

THAT'S WHAT I thought one morning which went terribly wrong. Here's how it started: just like every morning, my alarm clock went off at 5:00 a.m., and I jumped out of bed with my gym clothes on. I grabbed my cell phone and went outside for my morning walk. I was about halfway through my walk when a downpour began. My first thought was I needed to keep my cell phone dry. I immediately took my shirt off, wrapped my phone in it, and put it into the front pouch of my shorts.

I was several miles from home and realized there was nothing I could do, so I decided to continue practicing my speeches and body language like I do every morning while talking to myself.

After a few minutes into my shirtless pouring-rain routine, I noticed a Ford Mustang with its emergency flashers on about fifty feet behind me. With every step I took, the car followed behind.

After about ten minutes of being followed, I decided to turn around toward the car and walked right at them with my hands in the air, saying, "What do you want?" As I came within twenty feet, the car did an illegal U-turn and sped away.

I had no clue what that was all about. I was just glad the car wasn't still following me. I figured I probably wouldn't go for a morning walk outside ever again.

Another minute or so passed, and out of the corner of my eye, I saw that same Ford Mustang in the distance, doing another illegal U-turn and starting to come back toward me.

Suddenly, I saw two police cars speeding in my direction with their lights and sirens on. They stopped directly in front of me and pulled me over on the sidewalk.

The policemen got out of their cars in the pouring rain and looked at me. One police officer said, "What's going on?"

I said, "Thank goodness you're here. That Ford Mustang has been following me for ten to fifteen minutes, and I'm really concerned about my safety."

The policeman's response blew my mind. He said, "He called us on you! He said he saw a mentally deranged individual with no shirt on, talking to himself, using his hands, with a bulge in his shorts, which looked like it could be a weapon."

I was utterly speechless. It was the exact same situation with two completely different judgments.

The problem is we all see the world differently. Writer Anaïs Nin said, "We don't see the world as it is, we see the world as we are." In order to become the best version of ourselves, we need to attempt to put ourselves in the other person's shoes and see things from their perspective. And you know what? I did, and I did look a bit mentally deranged.

Instead of defending my situation, I put aside my truth to recognize the feelings of another person. My truth didn't change, but I chose to have an empathetic understanding for him.

Empathy is taking on another's perspective and feeling that person's feelings. This means putting aside what you think or believe for the sake of someone else.

The word *understanding* usually signifies knowing. But when empathy is linked up with understanding, the focus is no longer limited to knowing about that person, but it becomes about knowing that person's feelings and how that person perceives themself in the world.

Failure to develop empathic understanding leads to comparison, jealousy, arguments, and a lack of connection and growth.

Treading through today's world can be challenging. So many people have different values and beliefs, and sometimes it seems impossible to keep up and know how to respond or act in every situation to please all sides.

Many people say, "No matter what you do, someone will be offended or insulted." "Some people are just too sensitive." "Screw people." "Just be yourself, and you will find your tribe." "Once you do, you can be yourself and be happy."

The above statements are the easy way out and will never lead to growing to your potential. To develop yourself, having an empathic understanding of beliefs and values that aren't your own is vital. Learning, understanding, and accepting others where they are without trying to convince them differently takes serious work. In the beginning, you may insult someone accidentally. Growing yourself involves making lots of mistakes.

More importantly, finding forgiveness in yourself when you make a mistake always leads to growth. I make mistakes every day. Some mistakes are hard for me to swallow, but if I can learn from them, I become better. Sometimes I even need to apologize for my actions.

Rather than shutting down, gossiping, or belittling those with different perspectives, welcoming those who don't act or think like you is crucial for personal growth. Your opinion rarely convinces anyone to change their beliefs.

People may change their values and beliefs when inspired by others' actions or perspectives. By consistently living one's values and having an empathetic understanding for others that are different, it becomes possible to live harmoniously, opening minds to different perspectives and facilitating positive change.

I always thought it was my duty to push my view of the world on others and open their minds to what was happening. If everyone agreed with me, we could have world peace, the environment would be fixed, we would live longer and healthier, and everyone would be happy. I researched each of my beliefs and knew all the talking points and arguments to back them up. They became the truth. My truth.

I didn't have empathic understanding for others who thought differently. If I didn't understand or agree with their positions, I would secretly be glad when they were experiencing hardships. If my team won and their team lost, or their president lost the election, I would rub it in their faces. If they did something I disagreed with, I secretly hoped it wouldn't work out for them. Or if that super successful person finally had a failure, I would feel better about my own miserable life.

I didn't care what others with opposing viewpoints thought because I conditioned myself that the other side wasn't intelligent or didn't understand precisely how the world worked. They were misinformed. I was living in my bubble and yet not convincing others to change their views. I thought I was doing a service by opening everyone's mind. But I was doing a huge disservice to my own development.

Being outspoken, I was able to gain additional followers. People with the same beliefs as me teamed up to fight battles together. We would argue a point together on social media. I even became friends with some of my new followers. We would hang out and complain about the other side while distancing ourselves from the opposition as much as possible.

I settled into a pretty good life in my bubble. My bubble was made up of others who thought like I did. It was safe and felt nice. Initially, it felt good, but eventually, it led to dissatisfaction and a craving for more understanding.

As time passed, I started questioning why so many others had different beliefs and saw the world differently than I did. I was curious. Was I missing something? Eventually, I wanted to figure out how to be with others who didn't think or act like me. I wanted to ask them questions to understand, not to respond. I had refused to listen to the opposition my entire life, and realized it was limiting my growth. I wanted to explore and dig into their truth. Not the truth that had been ingrained in my brain for decades by where I grew up, what I read, and who I spoke to, but the other's truth.

I decided to change my ways. I started to seek out others who didn't think like me.

Eventually, I gained friendships with people who were nothing like me. In the beginning, I had some judgments. As I curbed my judgments and understood the opposition, I could free myself to gain the clarity I needed not only to see them as human beings but also to honor their life choices based on their lived experiences. This has been an incredibly freeing feeling.

As my friendships started to evolve, so did I. It was fun getting to know others who had different views than I did. As more and more time passed, I was determined to find ways to bring together differing viewpoints in the name of humanity.

> *It was fun getting to know others*
> *who had different views than I did.*

For my fortieth birthday, I gathered a group of around twenty friends from different backgrounds for a weekend in Atlantic City, New Jersey. I invited Republicans, Democrats, anti-governments, Catholics, Jews, atheists, bisexuals, people of color, Caucasians, those of different income levels, vegans, meat eaters, people who drank alcohol, and others who were sober. The weekend had the potential for disaster.

During one of our first meals together, I stood up and said I was thankful everyone came out for a weekend of fun. I said I would like to make two requests. First, we all come together for dinner each night. Second, we get to know each other. I said we have many differences, but if we could have a conversation with someone different than us, that would be the best birthday present I could receive.

The group was fantastic and has taken a life of its own. We have a group text message chain that supports one another, jokes with each other, and counts down the days until the next trip. Don't get me wrong: there have been debates and disagreements, but they are all respectful, and that is a massive step in the right direction. I'm so blessed this group of guys was willing to take a chance on what I was trying to accomplish. The group continues to grow each year, which is highly satisfying.

HOW TO DEVELOP EMPATHIC UNDERSTANDING

1. Become Sensitive

Become aware of what others may be sensitive to—understanding the events that led them to this path. It doesn't mean it is good or bad; it's just seeing the world through another person's lens.

In the past, I struggled with being sensitive to what was important to others. I recall organizing a birthday dinner with friends, reserving a table at a steakhouse I had been eager to try. However, two attendees were vegan. I assumed salads would suffice for them, failing to truly understand or care much about their dietary preferences. This oversight affected my relationships with them. The next year, I opted for a vegan-friendly restaurant, and I noticed an improvement in my connections with those friends.

Becoming sensitive to what is important to others involves getting to know or understand another's views and being mindful of those decisions. Realize this isn't about you, but about learning and exploring motivations of others who think or act differently.

Talk about common interests and be open to a different perspective.

Below is a two-sided example to reference sensitivity around different views. Just because you are sensitive towards another doesn't mean others will be. Keep being the change you want, release your ego from what you thought it should be, and accept what it is.

> **SIDE ONE:** If you are going to dinner with a hard-core vegan friend, choose a vegan-friendly place. Stay away from talking about the fish you caught and fileted.

> **SIDE TWO:** If you are vegan, let others order and eat their meals without making them feel bad or guilty. You will never convince someone to become vegan by belittling their meal choices. If they want to explore veganism, they will see how you live your life, research it, ask questions, and then decide if and when it is right for them.

2. Get Over Yourself

Recognize there are knowledgeable people who don't see the world the same as you. Just because you are intelligent doesn't mean your view is the correct view. Your life choices, who you associate with, and your upbringing play significant roles in your evolution. As soon as you get over yourself, you will see the world differently and be open to how others see it.

3. Be Open

If you want to understand others, listen and learn without forming a judgment. Fight the urge to respond and try to convince others you're right. Be aware that you don't know all the answers and adopt a beginner's mindset.

4. Ask Questions

This will free you from all your old judgments and allow you to understand someone else's perspective. Asking questions is an opportunity to humanize another and know why they feel a certain way.

5. Bring Together Others Who See Life Differently

To reach your potential, you must form relationships with others that are different from you. That is where learning and true growth takes place. I believe the ultimate goal in life is to empower others to reach their desired success. Being closed-minded to others who see the world differently limits your ability to empower them. Open your mind to the possibility of another way while attempting to make a real difference in this world.

If you want to be the change instead of talking about change you need to climb the rungs of the Empathic Understanding Ladder.

THE EMPATHIC UNDERSTANDING LADDER

First Rung: Empathic Understanding for Others Who Are Suffering

If you can't have an empathic understanding for someone who is suffering, you're probably struggling in many areas of your own life.

Supporting someone suffering from family loss, illness, or recent misfortune shows you genuinely care and develops your character. While possessing empathetic understanding alone doesn't guarantee lasting fulfillment, lacking it gives no chance for fulfillment.

Slowing down to be with someone who is suffering, listening to them, and putting yourself into their shoes to attempt to understand what they are going through will make a massive difference in that person's life as well as your own.

Many times when someone has a misfortune, others rationalize the reason for their suffering. They have cancer because they smoked, they had a heart attack because they ate poorly, or they are poor because they never took a chance. There is no benefit to having these reactive judgments, which is discussed further in chapter 7, "Be Observant." It doesn't matter what events lead to someone's suffering, but having an empathic understanding will always lead to the development of your character.

I want to be clear about something. Although empathic understanding involves attempting to understand another's point of view, it's not an open invitation to drain all your energy and well-being. If others continuously complain about their miserable lives or constantly talk about all the minor health problems they are having, finding a balance that works for you while allowing the other to be who they are is key. No one wants to hear about all your issues every time you speak. The more you complain, the more complaining you do. It is highly addictive. Nobody likes to go to a pity party. Surrounding yourself with positive, supportive, growing people will develop your character and propel you to better health, relationships, and more success and fulfillment.

Second Rung: Empathic Understanding for Others Who Are Celebrating

How do you react when you hear of others having joy? Whether they posted how much fun something was, how happy they are, or how fortunate they have been, do you get jealous? Awareness, when your emotions shift to jealousy or frustration, can open your eyes to the real reason you have this feeling.

Maybe you're feeling down about your own life. Each time you experience jealousy or frustration, it's a chance to get to know yourself better. Each time you express your jealousy or frustration internally or externally, you are not allowing yourself to build noteworthy relationships and develop yourself.

Having empathic understanding when someone is celebrating replaces jealousy with joy. Not just half-ass joy. People can smell phony miles away and can read your jealousy and frustration. To change your world, switch from jealousy to compelling joy and watch your life go from suffering to succeeding and fulfilling. In the beginning, you may have to push yourself into being joyful. But when you make it, you will see others' successes as positives which will propel you forward. Push yourself to become completely authentic and celebrate others' successes. It will multiply and affect those who are in your path.

Furthermore, it's great to celebrate. I know many people who hold in their joy for fear of making others jealous and don't want to rub their successes in another's face. I'm here to tell you that celebrating is excellent and essential.

By holding a celebration in, you are saying to yourself and others that it isn't okay to be happy or excited to have success. When you train your brain to celebrate, it gets used to feeling good, and the neural pathways associated with it strengthen.

Celebrating victories is important—whether small or big. The more wins and celebrations you have, the more successes and momentum you will have, and in the process, others will feed off your energy, causing those around you to win.

Be careful not to brag when celebrating. There is an overlap between celebrating and bragging, and if you plan to develop your character, celebrate by using gratitude, not by belittling someone else. Stick to the facts and give credit to the others who made that success possible. Any monumental success is only achieved alongside others.

Third Rung: Empathic Understanding for Those Who Don't Want to Do What We Want

What do you do when your partner or friend doesn't want to do something you want them to do? Do you try to make them feel bad or guilty? Do you accept it? Is your happiness dependent on how others respond?

Accepting another's decision or actions will give you the freedom to move through life, observing and loving others for who they are.

That may sound very difficult to most of you because most believe, if others don't do what we want, it will affect us.

If your partner doesn't want to go to see the movie you want to watch, will it affect your mood? If your friend cancels at the last minute, will it affect how you feel? Your happiness is not dependent on others. Ask someone else to go or go by yourself.

You are in complete control of your destiny.

Fourth Rung: Empathic Understanding for Others with Different Beliefs and Values

Do you find yourself distancing yourself or waging war against others who don't see the world the same as you? Do you belittle them for having a different view? Do you make fun of them? Do you distance yourself from them?

If you have a long enough conversation with anyone, you will realize we are all quite different.

Does your lack of understanding of another's beliefs and values frustrate or scare you, causing you to bash, belittle, or dismiss it? When was the last time you conversed with someone of an opposing viewpoint? Was it a back-and-forth, heated, persuasive argument? Empathic understanding is grasping how another came to this point in their life—listening to understand, not to object. We were all raised differently and have lived different experiences, which causes us to see everything in unique ways. Being open to others' views that aren't yours will open your mind to a larger purpose and compliment your character in the process.

You may say, "How will we live in harmony unless I convince others of my belief?"

When was the last time you were able to convince another their belief was wrong and yours was right? The answer is probably never. You cannot convince someone to change his or her mind about a belief. Getting to a place where you understand others' opinions and accept them with no need to judge or attempt to convince them to change means you have successfully climbed the fourth rung of the Empathic Understanding Ladder.

It's a common misconception that having empathic understanding for another person with an opposing viewpoint means you would be compromising your true self. You can live your life however you want, but doing it at another's expense will limit your character growth.

Being Catholic doesn't mean you can bash atheists. Be pro-Catholic. Being a Democrat doesn't mean you can attack the Republicans. Be pro-Democrat. Being athletic doesn't mean you can criticize others who are overweight. Support a healthy lifestyle. If you want to grow yourself, live your message every day.

Fifth Rung: Empathic Understanding for Others Not Credible

How do you respond when others don't do what they promised?

Do you review the situation with them, hoping they can grasp what happened and make it right? Do you give them a second chance? But when you do, the same thing happens repeatedly, and they never get it. They may not even recognize they didn't do what they said they would. Furthermore, they genuinely believe they didn't do anything wrong, and no amount of convincing will change their minds. You want to make them aware of the mistakes they made or changes they need to make in the future to be better, but you think they are either too stubborn or need more understanding to prevent the same situation from happening again. You try to hold in your frustrations, but you are at your breaking point.

If that sounds like you, know this. It's not up to you to explain your level of understanding, hold them accountable, or motivate them to be who they agreed to be. All of this frustrates you and makes you want to beat your head against the wall.

You have two options. First, you change your mindset and accept this person as they are, or second, create boundaries. This could mean limiting your time with them, developing new safe boundaries, or ending all ties.

The situation isn't magically going to go away, stop occurring, or stop affecting you, and it is not your job or in your best interest to continue to bash them to teach them a lesson. The longer you wait, thinking the situation will improve, the more negativity builds up inside.

The goal is not to unload your emotions on them, gossip about them, or make their lives miserable. Changing your mindset, cutting ties, or creating boundaries that benefit you will allow you to build the strong relationships you need.

As you move into your new self, find forgiveness in your heart, even if they don't apologize, so you can move on. Do it now. Do it for you. The longer you put off forgiveness, the longer you will suffer.

Let's say you ask a friend to go on vacation with you and they agree to let you know the next day. When the next day comes, they still have not responded. Don't waste your time or energy getting frustrated with them. Have an empathic understanding that they may have forgotten. That doesn't mean you need to ask them again and remind them if you don't want to. Based on your emotional needs, you may think twice before asking that person the next time.

Just note that life is full of disappointments; if you sever complete ties with everyone who has done you wrong, you may not have anyone left. That is why this book is so important. It guides you to lead by example, which will cause others around you to grow.

Sixth Rung: Empathic Understanding for Others Who Are Judging You Negatively

How do you react when someone makes a negative judgment toward you? Do you allow your ego to defend yourself? Do you allow them the power over you?

People who judge you negatively are doing so based on their life experience and their place in life at that point. Just because someone is judging your life doesn't mean their opinion is true. You are the only one who gets to determine your truth. Don't allow others the power over you because you will spiral out of control and fall into a useless place. The pity place. Pity is the worst negative trait you can own, and nobody wants to be around someone who feels sorry for themselves.

The next time someone judges you negatively, don't allow that individual control over you. Realize that person is either struggling or has not developed their own character to have enough awareness of what they are doing. Furthermore, it is not up to you to point these negative remarks out to another. If you do, you have allowed your emotions to control your outcome. It becomes a battle between two people with too much ego and too little self-control, which will surely not end the right way.

The next time someone calls you out negatively, take a breath, process what is happening, and realize, if you want to master this rung, you must understand and accept another's perspective and not allow them to take you out of alignment.

Seventh Rung: Empathic Understanding for Others Who Hurt You

You might ask how you can forgive the person who destroyed your world.

They have chewed you up and spit you out to suffer more. They could be trying to sabotage you.

Having empathic understanding for someone who has hurt you is undoubtedly the highest rung of the ladder for a reason. Coming to a place where you can understand the events that lead someone to hurt you can open your mind and give you the closure you need in order to move on.

They may have hurt you because of their lack of mental development, how they were raised, a chemical imbalance, or their lack of understanding of others. This doesn't excuse them for what they did.

They may have destroyed your life and caused you to start over, become frail, unconfident, and in constant pain.

Getting to a point where you can understand the events that led them to this point in their life will free you from all the demons weighing you down. In the process, you will understand and realize your true strength.

You deserve to live a full life of growth, healing, and understanding. By allowing the pain to overtake your world, you give control and ownership over to the person who caused it. You are the owner of your destiny. And just because someone came into your life and flipped it upside down doesn't mean you have to stay down. Take back your life.

You can continue to have limited fulfillment and endless frustrations, or unlimited fulfillment and inner peace by adopting an empathic understanding mindset.

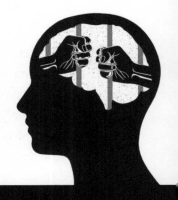

CHAPTER 5

BE ACCEPTING

When expectations increase, personal fulfillment decreases.

I can't believe they didn't call me on my special day. Some friends they are!

THAT'S WHAT I thought each time my birthday rolled around and I didn't get acknowledgment from family and friends.

I'd always look forward to my birthday to feel the love from others. The social media birthday messages, texts, calls, and the joy of opening cards and presents from friends and family all added to the excitement of my special day.

Then, at the end of the day, I would analyze and report on how others responded to my birthday. Their actions caused me to judge our relationship accordingly. Others were unknowingly competing against my expectations of them.

I would say, "I never got a text from my buddy saying he is thinking about me on my special day."

On top of that, I would analyze the presents I got. Most of the time, the presents weren't good enough, and the messages in the cards weren't thoughtful enough.

I mean, I not only wanted to feel special, but also to know that your world revolved around me. Year after year, my birthdays were filled with disappointment and unrealistic expectations, which led me to never look forward to or enjoy having them.

Several years ago I chose to let go of those expectations, because I didn't want to continue living that way. Shifting my focus to the positive aspects of my life, I acknowledged that the world didn't revolve around me, and others weren't intentionally being hurtful by not meeting my perceived demands. In most cases, others had no clue what my expectations were. For the first time in my adult life on my birthday, I decided to have fun. I curbed my actions to not talk of what didn't happen on my birthday; instead, I talked about what I did and what was great. I went to play a round of golf and had a blast. I released all expectations of others.

Every frustration stems from a *personal* expectation. Each time you choose a negative emotion, it's a moment where happiness is lost. Your fulfillment relies on letting go of expectations.

> *Each time you choose a*
> *negative emotion, it's a moment*
> *where happiness is lost.*

What personal expectations do you have?

Do you expect the family Thanksgiving celebration to go a certain way? Do you expect to have a short phone conversation with a friend? Do you expect your spouse to ask about your day? Do you expect your kids to come for a visit on holidays? Do you expect to get a raise or a bonus each year? Do you expect someone to call you back within a certain time frame after you call? Do you expect your coworkers to say good morning? Do you expect to receive a certain birthday message? Did you expect your book to be done by now?

How do you respond when your expectations aren't met? Do you feel bad, or try to make the other person feel guilty, or dismiss them because they aren't good enough?

Just because it used to be a certain way doesn't mean it is that way anymore. Allow others the freedom to live the life they choose by supporting them, even if you don't agree with or understand them.

EXCEPTIONS TO EXPECTATIONS

There are *only a few* scenarios where an expectation can prove positive.

In your job, career, project, or education. In this case, it's beneficial not only to meet expectations but also to *exceed* them. Examples include exceeding a teacher's expectations of an assignment or going above and beyond expectations for your customers, your boss, or your team.

When you are voluntarily participating in something that has rules. Some examples include: going on an airplane, following the speed limits, attending an event, or following the direction of a guardian who has made a decision.

Otherwise, expectations are a formula for disaster. If you catch yourself having an expectation of someone, I encourage you to be the catalyst for change rather than convincing, gossiping, or withdrawing from the relationship. Invest more effort in personal growth and proactively make the changes required to adapt to the evolving relationship. Once you take ownership of yourself and let go of expectations, you'll pave the way to live the life you desire, ultimately strengthening all your relationships.

There are *three types of expectations*. Expectations of self, another's expectations of you, and expectations you have of others. As we dive into each, ask yourself which type of expectation you are most prone to.

Do you set expectations for yourself? Do others place expectations on you? Are you likely to impose expectations on others? To minimize disappointment, frustration, and strained relationships while building your character, it's essential to let go of expectations. When you do, you can be at peace and harmony while building solid relationships.

1. Expectations of Self

When you put expectations on yourself, you are attached to the outcome. This can lead to overwhelming pressure, causing "destination disease," where you believe the more you do or the faster you go the happier you'll be. You are delaying your happiness until a future date. Consider shifting from rigid expectations to setting intentions, allowing flexibility in your journey. Intentions direct your mind to the plan and habits to kick-start you toward your future self.

**Expectations focus on the destination,
where intentions focus on the journey.**

I believe it's important to know where you are going, but as life gets complicated, or things don't go as planned, expectations are a setup for disappointment. It's about embracing the journey and being open to different outcomes, not your perceived failure when situations don't go exactly as planned. Trying to control a situation is extremely difficult. Releasing expectations allows more flexibility and openness to the possibility of a different, or maybe even better, result.

Example: Do you expect to lose twenty pounds before your wedding? While having the goal of getting in shape and improving health is commendable, fixating on a specific weight-loss target sets a destination, creating an expectation. Instead, focus on developing lasting habits for lasting results. Many individuals regain lost weight because they believed they arrived, leading them to indulge.

> *"People do not decide their futures,
> they decide their habits, and their
> habits determine their future."*
> —F. MATTHAIS ALEXANDER

2. Another's Expectations of You

Remember that someone else's expectation of you is theirs, not yours—and therefore, it is their problem, not yours. I understand that you might feel compelled to react because of guilt. They are trying to make you feel bad so they can feel better. You are not responsible for another's expectations.

I used to be that person. I tried to make others feel guilty for not doing what I said. Sometimes I was successful in having them change, and sometimes I wasn't. If I wasn't successful, I would double down and hold a massive grudge against them or stop speaking to them, which drained not only my energy, but also theirs. I didn't care that much about my energy. As long as I was able to exert influence over theirs, I was winning. I believed this would lead to my ultimate power. I was convinced I knew best for everyone.

If I was successful in manipulating them into meeting my expectations, they weren't happy. They built up anger toward me and distanced themselves from me. Frequently, others would erupt with frustration because I insisted on telling them how to be.

The best medicine for someone who attempts to manipulate you, just like my past self, was simply saying no, without an explanation. You command control of your life. If you don't control your life, someone else will, and guess what they have in store for you? Not much. You don't owe anyone an explanation of why you are choosing not to meet an expectation. If you have no desire to do something, don't do it, as simple or as difficult as that may sound. This may cause your relationships to change. This may cause you initial pain. I know the person could be a close family member or a great friend, but each time you allow them to dictate your actions, you are saying you don't value yourself. The more you unwillingly meet others' expectations, the more they will willingly expect more. This is a vicious cycle that burns you out and holds you back from becoming who you want to be.

Take control of your life. As you do, some will respect you, some will drop off, but everyone will realize you are now taking charge of your destiny.

Does someone expect you to give or lend them money? Is someone attempting to exert control, pushing you into something you don't want to do?

If you let a friend or family member borrow money, how would you feel if they never pay you back? Are you content with letting go of the money, or does it bring mental or emotional stress? If you do let another borrow money, release it, and don't expect anything in return.

Relationships always get tricky around expectations. Remember you are in ultimate control of your decisions, and don't let others attempt to guilt you into meeting their expectations.

If you say no, the relationship could go sour, but if you say yes, it could affect your well-being. Furthermore, by agreeing to an expectation, you increase the odds of them asking for more in the future. Dive into your personal emotions before you give into another's expectation. The only way to successfully navigate the difficult expectations others put on you is to release the emotions and feel good about your decision.

Expectations by Default
Household responsibilities are often distributed by default, with many accepting their roles. However, when challenges arise, these responsibilities can become unclear, and external expectations may surface. Through open communication and a team mindset, you find solutions.

My wife naturally took on tasks of buying our kids' clothes and going grocery shopping. I took on the trash duty and making the family breakfast and lunch. We never explicitly discussed these responsibilities but committed to being a team, fostering open communication to address any overwhelming situations and find solutions.

3. Your Expectations of Others

You may not even realize you have expectations of others. An effective way to gain awareness of the expectations you put on others is by reflecting on your past day or week and answering these three questions.

1. What did I ask of others?
2. How did I respond if those expectations weren't met?
3. Did I talk negatively about another person because he or she didn't fulfill my expectations?

Here are some action steps designed to eliminate your expectations of others:

1. *Do it yourself.* The simple way to eliminate expectations of others is by learning to do something new.
2. *Pay someone to do it for you.* Paying someone puts value on what you want.
3. *Ask another to empower you.* People find joy in empowering others to achieve their desired success. While they may not want to do it for you, they often provide the answers so you can do it yourself. Your future depends

on your efforts. Anything of value in life requires work. Learning and growing makes you better, and the more you implement what you learn, the greater your success, leading to fewer expectations of others.

Adjusting to Change

Has your relationship with a loved one changed because they changed, or they refuse to change, or expectations have changed?

They used to be more loving, caring, and affectionate. They used to do more for you. It's almost like they don't appreciate you.

It is clear as day that the relationship is deteriorating because of them. For any chance of improvement, they would need to apologize and revert to the person they used to be, aligning with your expectations.

Wrong. That was my view for most of my adult life.

The flaw with that mindset is you cannot change anyone else. Convincing or attempting to force someone to do something may provide temporary compliance but will never create lasting change. The key lies in changing oneself.

Relationships are constantly evolving. If you don't release your expectations of the other person, you can never grow into the newly defined relationship. I know you believe you are just attempting to help them. But each time you accept others for who they are, instead of what you think they should be, you allow them to become who they genuinely want to be while relationships remain in harmony.

When expectations increase, personal fulfillment decreases.

Your demands will never create lasting success. Lasting success is found in ways to learn and grow instead of blaming others for your failures. When faced with challenges, focus on how to become better, and don't rely on others to change.

Expectations are the reason marriages fail, relationship fallouts occur, health deteriorates, and success is limited. When you release expectations, you get to decide the life you want to live.

Suppose you're navigating life without a clear direction, experiencing recent failures, or finding yourself falling short of where you want to be. In that case, there's likely a tendency to heighten your expectations of others and, in the process, bring them down as an attempt to lift yourself up.

Many of us hold expectations of the government, relationships, jobs, and financial situations. However, expecting others or a situation to conform to your desires won't give the lasting outcome you would like. The only thing your expectations do is build your frustrations.

Real change occurs by living your message and allowing others to live theirs. If they see your message as the change they choose, they can choose to change.

Climb the rungs of the Expectation Ladder and let go of expectations to cultivate a more fulfilling mindset.

THE EXPECTATION LADDER

First Rung: Identify Your Expectations

Identifying expectations involves paying attention to your thoughts, emotions, and behaviors. Notice moments of frustration, disappointment, or surprise during your interactions with others. Ask yourself if these reactions stem from unmet expectations. Maintain control over your external demeanor as you analyze the situation. Focus on recognizing the positive aspects of others and regulating your outward expressions. Understand that delaying your emotions allows you to influence the outcome. Reacting to unmet expectations never yields a positive outcome.

Journaling or discussing your feelings with a trusted confidant can offer insights into your expectations. When gaining guidance, steer clear of gossip and concentrate on personal growth. Developing self-awareness is crucial to identifying and managing all expectations.

Let's say you walk in from a long day of work and notice the trash can overflowing. Your insides begin to boil, and you're ready to react. You wonder why your partner can't take the trash out. You begin to form a story in your head, and you're ready to blow up at them. As you react, they defend themselves, stating it is your responsibility and they were busy taking care of the kids all day.

You and your partner are now fighting, and nothing positive has come from your reaction to your unmet expectation.

If you identify your emotions as they begin to come in, then you can take a deep breath and accept them as they are without reacting. While initially challenging, each time you delay your reaction, you are training yourself to be calm. When you remain calm, you respond correctly, and it always leads to controlling the outcome.

Second Rung: Change Your Mindset

Changing your mindset around expectations involves shifting from a rigid and fixed outlook to a more open and adaptable approach. It means recognizing that life is inherently unpredictable and not everything will unfold exactly as planned. Instead of setting specific, inflexible expectations, you cultivate a mindset that is more accepting of various outcomes.

In essence, changing your mindset around expectations is about fostering adaptability, resilience, and a more positive perspective, which can lead to greater satisfaction and contentment in various aspects of life.

This involves removing all assumptions you have. By assuming, you believe you know the answer. It may be your truth but another's lie. Challenge yourself to have a beginner's mindset and be open to your own growth. As you do, you open your mind to many avenues and allow the universe to bring you more harmony and success.

By assuming your partner knew to take the overflowing trash out and had the time to do it, you thought you understood their situation better than they did. Your relationships will suffer any time you have an assumption that you react to.

Third Rung: Know Your Direction

Clearly defined goals, when paired with purposeful strategies and habits, have the power to eliminate expectations, offering a more focused and intentional framework.

In essence, defining goals shifts the emphasis from anticipating specific outcomes to actively working toward personal aspirations. It encourages a mindset of growth, adaptability, and proactive engagement, ultimately reducing the impact of unmet expectations.

Fourth Rung: Plan Ahead

If you know where you want to go, you can envision the future and effectively plan ahead, which takes the pressure off the situation and naturally releases expectations.

It takes time to prepare and think about potential obstacles and how they could be overcome. Lack of planning on your part doesn't constitute an emergency on my part. By preparing, you attempt to cover all bases and uncover all rocks with the mission to achieve without expecting or assuming.

When making repairs around the house, I fail to plan appropriately quite often. I think a task will take an hour, but it winds up taking two. On top of that, I don't always plan correctly. I run to the hardware store, buy what I think I need, and come home only to realize I forgot something else and need to run back again. This process has caused me a lot of grief and frustration. I expect to get the job done in the time frame I allot, but when I fail because of my lack of planning, it always leads to a ripple effect that affects the entire day.

Fifth Rung: Control Your Actions

What is your objective when asking someone to do something for you? Are you too lazy? Are you too busy? Does someone else know how to do it faster or better? If your relationship is built on asking others to fulfill your needs, you allow them to own you.

Instead of going down the path of self-pity, the "please help me" road, control your actions and carve out time to learn something new.

If you feel negative emotions start to surface, take a deep breath and count to ten.

Sixth Rung: Give Gratitude

Gratitude can shift your perspective and bring attention to the positive aspects of a situation. Gratitude concentrates on what you have rather than your shortcomings. Giving gratitude will release expectations by naturally building a community of friends based on who they are, not who they are not. It encourages you to appreciate the present moment and the positive aspects of what's going on around you.

By releasing expectations, you can manage disappointment. When expectations are too rigid, any deviation from the anticipated outcome can lead to frustration or disillusionment. By removing expectations, you are better equipped to handle unforeseen circumstances.

Unreasonable expectations can lead to stress and anxiety. When you approach situations with a more open and adaptable mindset, you're likely to experience less emotional turbulence, promoting a healthier mental state.

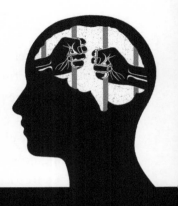

CHAPTER 6

BE HONEST

When you tell the truth you have nothing to remember.

Nobody will never find out the truth. I'm not lying, really.
I even have this fantastic medal to prove my win.

THAT'S WHAT I told myself after winning first place in the masters (over forty) men's physique category at the East Coast All-Natural Bodybuilding competition in Fort Lee, New Jersey, in June of 2021 at the age of forty-three. That win is what I blasted out to my friends and family on social media.

This competition took place during the downswing of the COVID-19 outbreak. The day of the competition arrived. I entered three different categories: Novice Physique, Open Physique, and Masters Physique. I was informed that the turnout of competitors was low due to the concerns of the pandemic. In fact, I was the oldest guy out there. In the first two categories, I was competing against kids half my age, and when the Masters contestants were announced, I realized I was the only competitor. I was competing against myself.

In the end, the judges announced the winners over the microphone, and I got to go on stage to get my hand raised as they put a first-place medal around my neck for competing and beating nobody but myself.

Did I lie to social media, friends, and family? Not really. But I wasn't telling the entire truth.

WHEN KEEPING A SECRET IS APPROPRIATE

In a few situations, being asked to keep a secret is essential:

- when a loved one shares their personal beliefs or values
- when someone is trusting you with their finances
- when a friend is discussing a health concern

Notice in these situations others have allowed you to come into their worlds to discuss themselves. They are trusting you with their own personal concerns that have nothing to do with anyone else.

These instances, along with navigating through the constant changes in a business or having the best interest in the well-being of a minor, are the only appropriate times to keep secrets quiet.

In all other cases, keeping a secret or telling a secret is a formula for disaster. Have you been asked to keep a secret?

Have you ever told a secret? If you're like me, that answer is an astounding yes.

I used to tell lots of secrets, and in return, people told me lots of secrets. Others would trust me with confidential information. That is why, when I told their secrets to others, I told them not to say anything. Sounds like a solid plan, right? I couldn't be trusted. I needed to be careful when telling secrets because my credibility would be ruined if that confidential information got back to the source. But if I honored that secret, I could be jeopardizing the well-being of someone else.

Many times, that person will find out that you were hiding a secret from them, which will jeopardize your reputation. It's not up to you to keep a secret, even if it is in their best interest. You are putting your credibility on the line each time you choose to tell or keep a secret. What do you do? Either way, you lose.

> *You are putting your credibility on the line each time you choose to tell or keep a secret.*

Stop telling secrets, and don't let others tell you secrets.

The next time someone asks you to keep a secret or withhold information from others, immediately cut them off; tell the person you don't want to be put into a situation where your character is challenged. If they choose to tell you anyway, you have a clear conscience and don't need to remember anything. If they try to make you feel bad, saying they need someone to vent to about a relationship or a situation, reverse the roles and ask them to be a good friend by not putting you in a situation without a positive outcome. Protecting your credibility is the most important thing you can do. Building a solid character takes years and could be ruined instantly. A true friend will accept your wishes.

Secrets are another form of dishonesty, and when dishonest people trust each other with secrets, guess what happens—more secrets. We then repeat the secret to someone else and tell them to promise not to say anything. This is a vicious cycle, and I lived it for many years.

I would say…

Don't tell the boss on me.

Don't tell anyone the truth about how much money I actually lost in Atlantic City.

Don't tell my girlfriend how much alcohol I drank last night.

Don't tell anyone I didn't find my golf ball, but I secretly dropped one in a good pin position.

Don't tell the kids that the Easter Bunny isn't real.

Don't tell him I told you his secret.

More lies.

My lies continued. Day after day, over and over. I inflated the truth, told secrets, and told lies to protect myself, to protect other's feelings, to make myself look better, and to cover up reality. I thought I would look better by lying or not telling the whole truth.

People always told me, "You have a great personality." I was so consumed with what a bunch of so-called friends and peers thought of me that I was living a fake reality, failing to become my best self.

I even embellished my fun stories that didn't need fluff and adjusted them to pump up my ego and make my personality look even better. I believed, if people liked me, I could eventually keep building relationships and gain more and more power.

I was so concerned with how others viewed me on the outside that I ignored what was happening inside. I was only interested in how I looked on the outside. The repercussions of not taking care of the inside started taking over and ultimately led to my credibility being tarnished. Others didn't trust me, questioned my character, lied back to me, and distanced themselves from me.

I would often contradict myself or get caught in my lies. This caused me to double down and go deeper into lies. I didn't remember who I told what to, which confused me. Mark Twain is often credited as saying, "If you tell the truth, you don't have to remember anything." I wish I had realized that sooner.

My stories would keep evolving and changing with just enough truth to keep them believable, but enough lies to make me look fun, exciting, and successful. I even bought a BMW Z4 convertible at age twenty-five, which I could barely afford, to build up my fake reality.

After a while, I would start to believe my own lies. I became a master liar. I told lies to myself and others enough times to convince myself I was telling the truth. When you believe your lies, you reach the pinnacle of your misery. Your life starts to spiral out of control.

My days were filled with lies; I noticed others would also lie to me. My relationships were consumed with lies, causing others around me to lie, which led me to gossip. "I don't believe a word they are saying to me," I would say. I was judging everyone's credibility but my own. I thought I was so good at lying, and others were so bad, that I would gossip about them not being truthful and always give myself the benefit of the doubt.

Then I met the most honest person I have ever known—my wife, Karen. She liked me because I was fun and exciting, but as time went on, she saw through my lies.

Karen was raised to always tell the truth. No matter what. It was her family's most important value. It was their family's foundational belief. It was hammered home to her as a child, and she was truly living her values. In the beginning, I didn't believe her words. I had no reason to. I thought most people were dishonest, and I didn't trust her. I had major trust issues and didn't have anyone in my inner circle I completely trusted. I was guarding myself because I didn't want to get hurt. But over time, and with a lot of internal work, I slowly shifted to honesty and trust.

If you need convincing that becoming honest will change your life, here are some of the most important reasons.

Honesty builds credibility. If you desire better relationships, you cannot sustain lasting fulfillment if you are dishonest. Credibility is gained through trust. It is only possible to be credible if you are trusted.

In a 2022 Gallup survey, the most admired trait of a professional was reported as honesty. In nearly every survey I researched on character traits, honesty came out on top, over and over. This means you can't have lasting professional success and build positive relationships unless you are 100 percent honest every time, even when it hurts.

Credibility allows relationships to develop and more personal growth to come into your life. They go hand in hand. To grow, you must be honest with yourself and others.

When you are honest, you will have nothing to remember. If you are like I was, I told bits and pieces of the truth to different individuals, but nobody got the entire truth. Who I was speaking to determined what lies I added to the story.

The problem was that I needed to remember what I told to whom, and if I had a group of people together who had heard different stories, it was extremely difficult to remember who knew what. Lying always catches up with you, leading to damaged relationships and ruining your credibility.

You cannot accept yourself if you aren't true to yourself. That means being honest. This will put you on the right path to discover your actual reality and see your future with a clear vision.

If life has you down, you are burned out from problem after problem, you're down on your luck and crying out, "Why me?" it's an opportunity to change your luck and become better. People who are consistently honest experience more good luck and better opportunities.

The repercussions of broken trust always lead to grief and eventually to anger. Why put yourself through that? You can change. You can be better.

Furthermore, if you lie, you possess one or more traits:

- *ego*: the need to feel special
- *fear-based emotions*: scared of being yourself for lack of acceptance of self and others
- *belief you won't get caught*: this is ego-driven

- *excitement*: lying is addictive, and receiving attention from all the drama you're causing can be exciting.

Some of the best liars I've ever met or best lies I've ever told all have one thing in common—the individual telling the lie is convinced the lie is true. They create a story in their minds of what happened, then rewind it and replay it over and over until it becomes their truth. If you are at this point, the recovery process isn't going to be fun or quick, but it will be the most meaningful thing you have ever accomplished.

After I became honest, I noticed my friendships started to shift, my luck began to change, more opportunities came my way, and my life started to change. Some friendships began to develop more, and others faded away.

In my experience, changing to honesty is challenging when doing it cold turkey. It's like any bad habit created over a period of time by making the wrong decisions over and over. The longer you have a bad habit, the harder it is to break. I had created such a bad habit of being untruthful over many, many years that I had lost control of myself and went deep into a depression.

Each day, our trust is consistently challenged. We are all put in situations where our credibility is on the line. Will you choose to live an authentic life or a fake one?

Trust is built by:

1. *What you say*: What are you saying to yourself and others?
2. *How you respond*: How do you react when others try to challenge and bring you their gossip?

3. *Your actions*: Are your day-to-day actions truthful, or are they leading others on?

It's time to break the habit of being the old you.

I'm excited to share how I grew and healed from a life of lies. Each day, I wake up fully energized with a clear mind, ready to develop more trusting relationships. My transformational process changed me, and others were impacted consciously and unconsciously for the better. As you begin to shift, you will notice others around you changing. You will see others in a new light, your surroundings in a different way, and you will begin to see a new beginning.

Climb the rungs of the Honesty Ladder.

THE HONESTY LADDER

First Rung: Awareness

The process of changing from untruthful to trustworthy begins with awareness. Call yourself out on the lies you're telling. At first, you may not feel comfortable coming clean or apologizing to the victims of your lie. Begin by forgiving yourself for the lie. Tell yourself you will do better next time. Come clean if you're feeling brave and want to propel this process. Yup, that's right, admitting you lied. That takes guts. It takes admitting you did wrong. You are throwing your already tarnished character on the line. But guess what? People eventually will forgive you as you become more reputable in the future. Credibility is built on honesty. Your consistent honesty will compound, and ultimately, your credibility will be repaired.

TIP: Journaling allows you to get out of your head. Free your mind. Write about the events that led you to the lie. This will bring awareness to do better next time.

Second Rung: Acceptance

If you want to make a change, accept that you have been inflating the truth, lying to yourself and others. Accept that your past lies created your present reality. Accept you have been wrong. The past is in the past, and forgiving yourself is part of acceptance. Free yourself from the lies you have told and start fresh.

Third Rung: Limiting Interactions

The process of coming clean from your life of lies can be similar to any addiction. Distancing yourself from the individuals who share the same addiction is critical to maintaining your well-being and recovery. Surrounding yourself with a supportive and positive environment can contribute to your efforts to break free and begin your recovery.

Do you have someone in your life that you can 100 percent trust? If you don't, I recommend hiring a life coach, a therapist, or reading a book on recovery. Some find truth through God while others join reputable organizations such as volunteering for a good cause in order to build a strong base. After a while, you won't be affected by your old buddy's lies. Your actions may even influence them to take the high road. But if they don't, there is a good chance you won't tolerate the lies and will find your relationship fading away.

As you become better, you will naturally manifest trustworthy, lasting friendships.

Fourth Rung: Accountability

Review your day. Who did you speak with? Was there anything you could have been more truthful about? Call yourself out. Ask a trusted friend if they can be your accountability partner. If someone can hold you responsible for your actions and call out your lies, it will likely motivate you to change your behavior.

As this book continues to uncover some of your truths, you get to make a choice. Will you choose an honest life that will transform you into the best version of yourself? I hope you do.

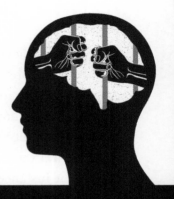

CHAPTER 7

BE OBSERVANT

It's okay to listen without having an opinion.

That is the worst call I have ever seen. I think this referee is intentionally trying to run up the score. I bet his daughter is on the other team.

THAT'S HOW I felt during my daughter's basketball game as I observed the opposing team's players and checked the score. The other team was significantly larger and taller than ours. They also handled the ball extremely well and made tons of their shots. The scoreboard didn't favor us, and as the game progressed so did the margin our team was down.

As I continued to observe, I started to evaluate the game in my truth. I believed the referee kept making ridiculous calls. All game long it seemed like he was purposely trying to run the score up for the opposing team. Our team was down by a ton, and he didn't give us one break. I decided to let the referee know exactly how I felt by letting him know all the calls he missed and expressing my disappointment for him ruining the game in my opinion. The referee came over, looked at me, and said, "I've had enough out of you." The opposing fans cheered as they thought the referee was doing a good job. Looking back on it, I was completely embarrassed.

In that instance, I chose to turn my observation into an evaluation expressing my opinion. What I have learned since then is just because I have an opinion doesn't mean it's right or everyone sees it my way.

Some of our opinions may serve to ensure our safety or provide valuable lessons while others hinder our openness to alternative perspectives. Our opinions stem from perceptions of our life experiences, and the conditioning we've undergone, and not all of them contribute positively to our understanding of a situation. Your opinion may be your truth but another's lie. When we act based on a belief something is fact, and it turns out it is not, this is when life can often go spectacularly wrong. Mark Twain has been credited with saying, "It ain't what you don't know that gets you into trouble. It's what you know for sure that just ain't so."

Think about all the opinions in the world during the COVID-19 outbreak. So many different opinions and truths were floating around about where it came from, the safety and effectiveness of the vaccines, mask policies, social distancing, and having social gatherings.

In the beginning, I was to blame as well. I was fighting the world to have them see it my way. The world was divided on so many levels and filled with hate and fear based on all the opinions around us. I heard many stories of families who used to be really close before COVID-19 only to have their relationships forever changed based on their perspectives that led to their judgments.

ALL EVALUATIONS ARE MADE-UP OPINIONS

Are you evaluating for self-improvement or safety, or are you evaluating to negatively judge?

There are instances when evaluation proves beneficial, particularly for self-improvement or safety. There are also instances where it does not. Distinguishing between when evaluations are essential for progress and when they lead to destruction is crucial. This is why I'm breaking them into two distinct categories:

1. ProActive Evaluation
2. ReActive Judgment

This will allow for a better understanding and enable positive changes resulting in a harmonious life. *ProActive Evaluation* is the ability to reflect, listen, and learn from a situation to understand without the need to display your opinion, unless directly solicited. It is where you can have the best interest of all parties in mind. These are positive evaluations that serve the purpose of improvement or to keep you or others safe. *ReActive Judgment* involves forming an opinion to belittle, gossip, or build yourself up while attempting to bring another down. These are negative and do not serve any useful purpose.

ProActive Evaluation

ProActive Evaluation relies on observation and having an open mindset. It eliminates the need to have a critique or feel the need to pick a side, ever. We give up the right to be right, while learning and growing ourselves. Having a ProActive Evaluation increases learning, connecting, and growth while decreasing arguments and stress levels.

Below are the instances where ProActive Evaluations prove beneficial.

1. ProActive Evaluation of Self

To enhance your life, it's crucial to be mindful of your choices and adapt when necessary. If ReActive Judgment arises, practice self-forgiveness, acknowledging that mistakes are part of being human. Learn from these experiences, enabling you to approach similar situations differently in the future.

Examples
- Evaluating your failing business to facilitate the necessary changes for self-improvement and advancement.
- Evaluating your performance in a speech to identify areas for improvement in preparation for the next opportunity.

2. Asking Another for a ProActive Evaluation

Requesting another's opinion, opening your mind, being receptive, and actively listening when seeking help are vital steps for personal advancement. This could come as a collaboration when deciding how to move forward.

Sometimes, we lack the awareness or skills for self-improvement.

Examples
- a coach or teacher mentoring someone
- asking another's evaluation of the book you are writing to improve it
- asking others' judgment of a political situation to gain clarity

3. Identifying a Role Model for a ProActive Evaluation
Look for others who have qualities you admire.

Role models offer an excellent starting point in defining the qualities you aspire to develop. Consider the qualities of your role models—which ones do you aspire to embody? Their work ethic, their skill, their personality, their leadership? Initiate a profound exploration of your awareness to discover the characteristics you admire in your role model. Identify ways to adjust your habits and propel yourself toward your desired destination by evaluating them and applying what you learn to your life.

Examples
- a president's ability to bring together both sides of the aisle and assessing their amazing leadership skills
- your coworker whose ability to communicate positively and connect during difficult times drives the business forward
- a successful business person giving advice about how to accumulate wealth

4. ProActive Evaluation for Physical Safety

In situations where physical safety is at stake, it's crucial to rely on your evaluation to respond appropriately and navigate the situation toward safety. It may be to defuse a situation, call for help, or offer assistance to someone you believe is in need.

Examples
- witnessing a car accident
- reporting a person walking into a deli with a knife in their hand and wearing a mask

All other evaluations fall into the **ReActive Judgment** category.

ReActive Judgments

ReActive Judgments usually involve a lack of understanding, leading to an unfair evaluation and conclusion. Having *ReActive Judgments* of people, places, things, or ideas doesn't serve any constructive purpose. Many individuals regularly have such judgments, often driven by various reasons such as coping with emotional pain, feelings of jealousy, a sense of inadequacy, or engaging in self-comparisons that result in negative self-worth.

To observe without evaluating is when one refrains from passing any ReActive Judgment. It encourages an open-minded exploration of the subject, allowing for a more profound understanding and a richer, unfiltered experience.

These ReActive Judgments are widespread. Parents assess their adult children's choices, assuming they know what leads to the best results. We critique celebrities for actions we deem unethical, engaging in gossip with friends. There's constant evaluation of beauty, success, possessions, and behavior. If we master our judgments, we free ourselves from our main enemy—ourselves. While eliminating ReActive Judgments completely is nearly impossible, it's crucial to understand that we aren't required to have an opinion. Not only that, but also it's our opinion that holds us back from making real, lasting changes within ourselves. When asked for your opinion, it's not mandatory that you give one. When another person is expressing a different viewpoint than yours, it's not necessary for you to point out the opposition. You could say, "I don't have an opinion," or "I understand how you can feel that way," while moving the conversation forward.

Furthermore, people frequently try to establish connections by judging others. Unfortunately, this often results in a false sense of bonding rooted in common insecurities. Making judgments like this increases the fear of being judged and weakens genuine connections.

Why do you engage in debates, judgments, or arguments? Is it to assert your viewpoint and convince others they are wrong? Is it to make yourself feel better? Your ego could be standing in the way of your well-being when attempting to convince others to be someone they are not.

There are *four scenarios* where we encounter ReActive Judgments.

Scenario Number One: Judgment of What Others Are Doing with Their Lives That Doesn't Affect You

Numerous individuals pass judgments on matters that don't directly impact them. The word that describes this best is *gossip*. Engaging in such judgments momentarily elevates self-esteem, providing a false sense of confidence. It fosters a perception of superiority with an attempt to gain reassurance and inflate a fragile ego. This boost allows them to feel more assured. However, going down this path is contagious and tarnishes your character.

Examples
- judging a friend's choice to move into a smaller house
- judging a close neighbor who is incurring debt by planning a vacation beyond their financial means
- judging another's habits

Scenario Number Two: Judgment of What Others Are Doing with Their Lives That Directly Impacts You

Even when faced with other's challenging choices that affect our lives, it doesn't give us the right to judge them for their decisions. Each person has their own life to live, shaping it through individual choices. While it can be challenging when someone close to you makes decisions you believe will affect your well-being, passing judgment directly to them can create barriers and may be hard to mend. Respecting individual freedom and having open communication without judgment can be more constructive in navigating such situations.

Examples
- a close friend or family member moving away
- a family member's decision to donate savings to charity instead of giving it to you

In order to have an outcome that will satisfy both sides, it's important not to hold a grudge and to make sure your emotions are in check before having a discussion.

Scenario Number Three: Solicited Judgment

Unless your career requires a ReActive Judgment, what is the point? When put in a situation where you are asked for or want to give your input, structure your response by asking questions. Turn it back on the individual instead of using it for an opportunity to feed your ego.

Examples
- Who are you going to vote for?
- Do you agree with what the boss said?
- What would you do if you were in my situation?

Scenario Number Four: Judgment of Self

Self-judgment is vital for personal growth, but it doesn't imply harsh self-criticism. Making mistakes is part of being human, and when you falter, it's crucial to forgive yourself. The key lies in recognizing those mistakes, forgiving oneself, and learning from them. Each misstep is an opportunity to gain awareness and choose a different path in the future. Be kind to yourself, acknowledging that growth involves understanding and evolving rather than dwelling on self-criticism.

Examples
- striking out at the big game
- blowing a job interview
- ruining a friendship

As you climb the rungs of the Observation Ladder, you will be able to turn ReActive Judgments into ProActive Evaluations.

THE OBSERVATION LADDER

First Rung: Discovery

Give yourself time to reflect on the situation to discover all truths. Pausing allows you to check in with yourself and understand everyone's emotions. When you slow down, it's much easier to dive into your inner thoughts, and as judgments arise, acknowledge and release them. Avoid expressing immediate judgments, allowing others the space to share their thoughts without evaluation.

Reflect on your day, considering moments where judgment crept in. The more awareness you cultivate around your opinions, the less you'll feel compelled to judge. Consider enlisting a close, trusted friend as your accountability partner to point out your Reactive Judgments and encourage self-reflection.

Second Rung: Incubation Period

This involves learning and listening instead of reacting and judging. Be open to what others have to say, even when it's not your truth. Keep your emotions in check as you open your mind to the other's truth. Letting the other's truth simmer leads to having an aha moment. That is when you gain the sudden realization of how to move forward without attaching a ReActive Judgment to it. You may say, *Life is busy; I don't have the time to let my emotions simmer; I need to move fast.* As you react, you will notice that reaction will cause the situation to take twice as long to resolve as it would by letting it sit and digesting how to move forward.

> *Be open to what others have to say,*
> *even when it's not your truth.*

Take time for yourself, pause, and breathe. Understanding and managing your emotions will lead to those profound moments of realization while eliminating the need to be right.

Third Rung: Don't Take the Bait

In situations where you are asked for an opinion or judgment, it's perfectly acceptable to excuse yourself or choose not to engage. Demonstrating empathy involves understanding the other person's feelings and showing compassion for their beliefs without feeling obligated to adopt a specific perspective on a particular topic. You could say, "I understand how you could feel that way," which shows empathy without choosing to participate in a side. This approach acknowledges the diversity of opinions and allows for respectful coexistence of differing viewpoints. It reinforces the idea that one can express understanding and compassion without necessarily embracing every viewpoint presented, giving way to an environment of open dialogue and mutual respect.

Fourth Rung: Remove Expectations of Self and Others

Release the burden of expectations, both from yourself and others. Recognize that the only person within your control is you. Freeing yourself from judgments grants you the choice to live each moment without being held back by preconceived notions. Allow yourself the space to be free from the weight of expectations.

When those expectations manifest themselves, allow them to come in briefly before releasing them internally. Catch yourself as you begin to evaluate negativity by saying, "Just stop!" No one benefits from your expectations.

Fifth Rung: Replace Judgment with Gratitude

As you elevate your inner vibe to gratitude instead of judgment, a transformative shift unfolds in your life, propelling you toward greater success. Judgments spawn negativity while gratitude embraces the positivity that invites success to become a natural companion on your journey.

The transformation from judgment to gratitude marks a profound shift in perspective. By letting go of the inclination to judge, we open ourselves to a world of appreciation and understanding. Embracing gratitude not only alters our internal landscape but also paves the way for richer connections and a more fulfilling life. It is through the lens of gratitude that we navigate a path free from the constraints of judgment, fostering compassion, empathy, and a deeper appreciation for the diverse tapestry of human experiences.

CHAPTER 8

BE SELF-ALIGNED

Words and Actions Aligned

Wow, seeing this guy so aligned makes me realize I have work to do if I want to truly live my message.

THAT'S WHAT I thought when I met Alan Miner-Berger, who goes above and beyond to make sure his actions match the words he uses and is my true inspiration for this chapter.

I met Alan in 2014; he was the director of my children's preschool. Each day when picking up my kids, I spoke with Alan and realized he was the first true environmentalist I had ever met. He didn't just talk about the change—he was the change.

He has been a vegan for over forty years. When I asked him why, he responded, "All of the reasons," including animal rights, health benefits, and environmental concerns.

Every product he uses and promotes must support his beliefs, including only buying cars that don't have leather seats, only purchasing shoes and sneakers free of horse glue, doing his best to avoid using plastic products, and not buying foods or products that contain chemicals. He rarely buys new clothes and reuses as much as possible. He makes every attempt to research and use products that support the well-being of the Earth. He isn't perfect but makes every attempt to do the best he can.

I had invited Alan to my fortieth birthday bash and was excited he was coming. It was his first visit to Atlantic City since he was a child. As we walked into the casino, there was so much to see. Lights were flashing, music was playing, bells were ringing, and people were dancing and having fun. It was beyond exciting. I remember the first thing Alan said, which completely blew my mind: "I wonder how many of the Earth's resources it took to build this place. I wonder how much energy this place uses. Everyone here drinks from a plastic cup, and I don't see one recycling trash can."

Out of everything to say at that moment that would have been the last thing I would have said.

He opened my mind to my lack of awareness and alignment. You see, I also talked about protecting the environment, but my actions didn't support it. I drank bottled water and didn't recycle, owned leather jackets, put fertilizer on my grass, bought lots of new clothing, and had a car that wasn't good on gas mileage.

Alan wasn't telling me how to be or what to do, but he opened my mind by living his values each day. His words and actions are in alignment, which has caused me to become more aware and try to live my message, just like Alan is doing.

Then a light bulb went on. I always thought it was my life's purpose to try to convince others their beliefs were wrong and to influence their thinking to align with mine. But you can't convince someone else to change their beliefs through debates and arguments. It took me forty years to understand that you must live your words if you want to create real lasting change and reach your potential.

Does what you say match what you do? Are you living out the mission you believe yourself to be on? It's much more difficult than you may think.

> *Are you living out the mission*
> *you believe yourself to be on?*

Most people don't even realize they are out of alignment, but it is one of the most important qualities of building a reputable character.

It's very easy to see others who are out of alignment based on our frustrations with them, boundaries you may have created, and contradictions they make. Many people in politics say one thing and do the opposite. You may see it with your family and friends as well. They say one thing, but their actions contradict their words. Telling others they are out of alignment is never a good idea. It isn't part of the solution. Support your messages by making choices grounded in your principles. Growing yourself involves aligning your words based on your beliefs and values and living those actions, even when it's tough. By doing so others around you will be impacted and start to live their own message.

To live your message and reach your potential climb the four rungs of the Alignment Ladder. Which rung is currently your most challenging?

THE ALIGNMENT LADDER

First Rung: Know and Trust Yourself

Who are you? Spend some quiet time with yourself each day, getting to know yourself. What is most important to you? What are you most passionate about? What are your core beliefs and values?

Alignment Traps

As you gather a sense of who you are, it's crucial to steer clear of the five *Alignment Traps* that will hinder you from living your best life and cause stress, jealousy, frustration, and limited success. Which traps have you caught up?

1. Awareness Trap:

I'm unaware I'm out of alignment.

Lack of awareness is the most common alignment trap. We want our situations to improve, but when faced with reality, we fail to make the changes to align our beliefs with our actions because of our lack of awareness. What are your beliefs? Why are these beliefs important to you? How can you live these values more consistently?

- Do you pride yourself on having a good relationship with your children or partner, but unconsciously make decisions that don't support that? What's one change you can make?
- Do you want to make a better life for your family, but don't know how? What is one small step that can start moving you on that pathway?

- Do you talk about protecting the environment for generations to come? What additional lifestyle changes can you adopt to live that message even better?

I want to encourage you to become aware of the changes to live your message more consistently. As soon as you become aware, you can take action and be on your way to the best version of yourself.

One of my highest values is to treat everyone with love and peace. I love getting to know others that are different from me and take pride in building relationships even when challenged.

However, when I notice an aggressive driver doing something unsafe, I naturally act more aggressively toward them. I won't allow them to cut me or others off, and I purposely try to add stress to their life. They are doing that to me, and I need to teach them a lesson.

When events like this happen, I realize I am out of alignment. My words don't match my actions.

It's official: as of today, I declare I will be kind on the road. So if you're looking for someone to cut off, please look for my car.

2. Financial Trap:
Money is more important than my alignment.
Money can force people to live outside their beliefs. Does money own you? What do you pick if you have the choice between money or aligning yourself?

Initially, you may choose money because you feel like your success is based on the amount of money you make. The problem with being caught up in the financial trap is you will always be chasing money, and there will never be enough. Real, lasting success and fulfillment depend on consistently aligning your finances with who you are.

- Are you working for a company whose mission you don't align with, yet you remain there because of the generous pay?
- Do you find yourself buying products from companies you don't align with because they are cheaper?

A good friend of mine revealed his struggles with the financial trap. His family has built strong values on eating healthy, exercising daily, and looking to lifestyle and diet changes for any sickness he or one of his family members may get. There are only a few scenarios in which they would use pharmaceutical drugs. Their thoughts on many pharmaceutical companies aren't the best. However, they are heavily invested in pharmaceutical companies in their stock portfolio. He struggles with this, but realizes it brings diversification to his investments, and he continues to benefit financially from companies he doesn't believe in. He admits he is out of alignment and fights with himself on how to handle it. Switching to investment strategies that are conscious of his beliefs could give peace of mind to live his message.

There are plenty of ways to align your beliefs and finances to maintain inner peace. Explore and adjust your life accordingly. In the long run, supporting what you believe dives into your passion, and that always leads to more success.

3. Time Trap:

There isn't enough time to live in alignment.

Do you control your time? Do you block out the time you need so you can be aligned? If you don't control your time, there is a good chance someone else will, and guess what they have in store for you. Not much.

Getting a hold of your time can be difficult. But failing to do so gives you no chance of maintaining a fulfilled lifestyle and attaining inner peace.

If this is you, try asking: What is something small and manageable I can do today to take back my time? If you value a healthy lifestyle, but don't make time for it, you are contradicting yourself and living out of alignment. Can you wake up earlier to exercise? Can you cut out the TV and go for a walk instead? Today is a good day to get started to control your time.

- Do you talk about how you love reading but fill in your free time watching Instagram reels instead?
- Do you want a new job, but don't make the time for that online course which will further your career?
- Do you pride yourself on a healthy relationship, but don't make the time to go to the therapist?

Time management will allow you to live your message more consistently. Carve out blocks of time, even if only a few minutes, to begin the process of living your true self.

4. Convenience Trap:

Convenience creates bad habits and takes you out of alignment.

We live in a world of convenience. Whether you value healthy eating, exercising, building a better business, or gaining knowledge, it is always challenged by convenience. There's the get-fit-quick workout to a magic six-pack abs, the magic diet pill to remove all the unwanted weight, the get-rich-quick businesses, or the fastest way to get a degree. The world dangles devils in front of us all the time. They may even provide temporary results, but lasting changes are built by living your message each day. After a while, your actions will catch up with your words as you begin to develop your future self.

If this is you, try to keep a mantra close, like "I will choose what is best over what is easiest."

I'm certainly guilty of this. I dabbled to make a quick million dollars when the government gave out the Employee Retention Credit (ERC) money to businesses to support them during the COVID-19 outbreak. Others around me were making crazy amounts of money as sales representatives helping businesses get their ERC money. I quickly signed up and got certified and contacted business owners to see if I could sign them up to get their ERC money. I earned a commission for each business I landed. I paused my career at that time as I tried to score some quick cash. But the more I pursued the ERC money angle, the more my reputation was affected in my other business. I became known as the man who jumped from one thing to the next, which ruined my credibility with myself and others.

5. Follow the Crowd Trap:
Everyone else thinks differently; I must change.

If you fall into this trap, there is a good chance you are a people pleaser. You lack the self-confidence and self-discipline to become who you want to be. You fear being unaccepted and alone.

If this is you, dive into your passions and make the changes to live your message. This may cause relationships to shift. Becoming who you want to be is hard, but as you do, you will feel free and won't have regrets. Your friends and family might surprise you and support your new passionate self. Start by doing or saying something small that puts you on your own pathway forward. This will kick-start you to have the confidence to make additional changes.

It's wonderful to care and not want to insult others' values or beliefs, but hiding your values for fear of not being accepted isn't a good idea and always leads to being someone you are not.

Examples of the Follow the Crowd Trap:
- When hanging out with a nonreligious friend, you insult your god to try to fit in.
- You buy a car you can't afford but want to keep up with your neighbors or family.
- You want to save money and stop drinking alcohol, but all your friends watch the game at the bar each week. You continue to live out of alignment.

As you begin to uncover all of your values and beliefs and discover how to live your message more directly each day, consider the following examples friends have given to me to reference their lack of alignment and action plans to live that message more consistently.

BELIEF	CURRENT ACTION/ OUT OF ALIGNMENT	CHANGED ACTION/ ALIGNMENT
I love animals.	I eat animals.	Become vegan.
I don't trust and would never use pharmaceutical drugs.	My investment portfolio includes pharmaceutical companies.	Change investment strategy.
I need to protect the environment.	I drink bottled water.	Get a water filter.
Diversity is important to me.	Upper management lacks diversity.	Promote and hire more diverse workforce.
I love my spouse.	I cheated on my spouse.	Become honest.
The government should do more.	I complain about government.	Become the change you want to see.

Four Tiers of Self-Alignment

In order to reach your potential, you must first gauge who you currently are. Which tier below currently describes the person you are?

The ultimate goal of self-alignment is to consistently examine our values and recognize how to make our actions more in alignment with them while honoring and respecting others' choices.

Tier One

Those who fall into this category have ***no values, no alignment, and no compassion*** for opposition. They are also not interested in becoming better.

They may be in survival mode.

They are usually frustrated each day and confused. They have no sense of worth. They have zero influence on anyone.

They only care about themselves.

Tier Two

Those who fall into this category **have values but no alignment and no compassion** for opposition. This level consists of people with certain beliefs but think they don't apply to them or are unaware that they aren't living them.

They may claim they care about others but don't show it. They belittle and want nothing to do with others of an opposing view. They live most days unsatisfied and lacking self-worth because life keeps knocking them down.

Tier Three

Those who fall into this category **have values and alignment but no compassion** for opposition. This group has strong morals. They possess a strong inner circle of others who think as they do and are confident in themselves. They are satisfied as long as others around them see the world the same as they do.

They often try to convince others to think like them. Their attempts to push their view on others limits their potential.

Tier Four

Those who fall into this category **have values, alignment, and compassion** for opposition. This group doesn't judge or tell others how to act or what to do. They let their actions speak for themselves. This group values others and often looks to others with different beliefs to learn lessons. This group has unlimited influence and inner peace.

Second Rung: Create New and Review Current Boundaries

If the same people consistently take you out of alignment, ask yourself what new boundaries you need to put in place to create a safe environment for your well-being. Do you need to limit the time you spend with someone to create a stronger mindset? As you navigate through your day, ask yourself if your boundaries need to be adjusted. As you grow, boundaries can be altered to ensure others will not affect you negatively, keeping your alignment intact.

For example, you may choose not to go outside with coworkers to socialize and smoke cigarettes when you are attempting to quit. Or if you are trying to live a more positive life you may need to limit interactions with others who consistently bring you down.

Ultimately no person should have power over you, but until you achieve that status, focus on your values and aligning them with your actions while maintaining safe boundaries.

Third Rung: Challenge Yourself

I love testing out my new growth by putting myself in situations that used to take me out of alignment. If you feel good about the person you have become and realize you can't control others, it's time to try out your new self. Challenge yourself by being present in those situations that have pushed your limits in the past. As you become better, others no longer have power over you. In the beginning, it is mentally draining to be around the individuals who pushed our limits. You may react. Forgive yourself and try again. As you consistently display self-control, aligning your values with your actions, you grow and evolve.

Coming to a place where you can let others be who they want while you grow is the most fulfilling place.

Fourth Rung: Grow Yourself

Live those beliefs consistently. When you're tired, hungry, or hanging out with the wrong crowd, living those values may be a challenge. You may want to cave into your old ways. But each time you do, your inner self is disrupted. Take control by staying on course instead of going back down the wrong path that will ruin your credibility and make you fall down the rungs. When you value your words and actions, you steer your own life and gain more fulfillment.

Examples
- When celebrating a friend's birthday you don't need to have a piece of cake and take your diet off course. Choose fruit instead.
- You have been working on becoming a better person, but you're tired and cranky and your partner said something that pushed your buttons. Allow your thoughts to come in and release them internally. Conflict is inevitable—battle is optional.

As you align your beliefs and actions, you experience more confidence and credibility, which in turn will lead to more wins in life. I am rooting for you.

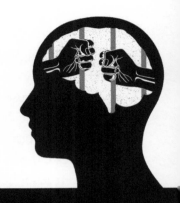

CHAPTER 9

BE CONNECTED

Connection is all about others.

How am I ever going to reach my goal of becoming a millionaire if I have to micromanage these incompetent employees? Nobody ever does the job right.

THAT'S HOW I felt when facing issues with employees at my commercial office cleaning business. I didn't understand that building relationships would influence them to work harder and go the extra mile for me. I believed others couldn't live up to my expectations. I believed that when they were on the clock, I owned them, and I didn't want to waste valuable time getting to know them.

As my company expanded, I found it challenging to be present everywhere. I observed that many members of my staff seized every opportunity to take advantage of the situation.

Customers complained, leading me to issue threats to my employees. Though there would be temporary improvements, they consistently reverted to the status quo, which was staff doing just enough to avoid termination. I refrained from connecting with my team because I was taught never to be friendly with them because when they screwed up, it would be more difficult to come down on them. I now recognize that I genuinely didn't grasp the significance that building connections would create the by-product of others working harder for me.

This is true for both professional and personal relationships.

Most individuals concentrate on themselves when communicating with others. They try to *connect* with others by speaking of their life, opinion, and/or experience but have no idea if their words will relate, insult, or even matter to the other person. They strive to connect to build relationships yet go about it all wrong. To guarantee a connection, you need to put others first. It doesn't matter if you are attempting to connect with a friend, family member, coworker, employee, or someone you just met. It's all about others.

If you want to have better relationships, make more sales, get promoted at work, become healthier, or have more wins in life, it's all about others.

Followers: Having followers doesn't guarantee success.

Merely holding a position of authority over others or having a substantial social media following doesn't inherently translate to ensuring enduring success.

It's a common misconception that the most successful individuals have the highest level of technical skills. Technical skills are the ability to do a job proficiently. People often assume that proficiency in a task equates to more successes. However, the extent of success isn't solely determined by one's knowledge. Consider the best connectors (a connector is someone who fosters relationships with the primary goal of enhancing the well-being and success of others). A common thread among them is the understanding that it's not about them but about others. While knowledge is valuable, true connection is what propels you further along the journey while developing who you are as a person.

Many organizations promote/hire the person with the best technical skills to lead an operation. Many online gurus have figured out ways to gain a massive online presence. But being an expert doesn't guarantee the ability to lead an operation to success and create a lasting impact. Failure to connect with others can curtail your progress and hinder potential achievements. Ineffectual connection may result in you working harder without extracting the full potential from those around you.

Ask yourself this: Are your followers listening to you because their lifestyle depends on it? Is there a paycheck attached to them following your orders? If you slow down and connect with your team, your relationships will improve, and they will actively want to do more for you.

The same is true for personal relationships. Concentrating on others will make them like you, want to be around you more, and be more willing to help you.

Numerous top professional athletes see their careers restricted when they focus solely on themselves rather than their teammates. The most successful professional teams consistently discover ways for their members to elevate each other. This principle holds true in life—your progress often hinges on how much you contribute to the well-being and success of others.

Ever wondered how some people effortlessly gather a team willing to go the extra mile for their projects or events while others with a great vision struggle to assemble a team?

The secret is connecting to others.

As you begin to gain a connection with others, it is your responsibility to demonstrate that you truly value them, you believe in them, and you live your message each day.

1. *To value another*: Spend time with them, listen to them without distractions, and show your appreciation toward them.
2. *To believe in another*: Trust them, empower them with responsibility, and foster their development, ultimately contributing to their success.
3. *To live the words you speak*: Your words and actions match. Are what you say you value and how you actually act the same? If you aren't sure, go back and review chapter 8, "Be Self-Aligned."

By consistently living these values, you give yourself the greatest opportunity to become the best version of yourself. The process may sound easy, but it isn't.

Think about your favorite teacher, author, friend, boss, or coworker. What is it that drew you to them? More than likely, it's because they cared about your success.

Connection isn't something you can start one day and expect to have results the next. You must climb the rungs of the Connection Ladder.

THE CONNECTION LADDER

First Rung: Connection to Self

**You can't effectively connect with others
unless you give to yourself first.**

I like the analogy of filling a cup. What do you need to fill your cup so you can pour into others? Once your cup is filled, you can pour into others. But if your cup is dry, you have nothing to give. Most people believe it is selfish to do something for themselves. But I'm here to tell you that unless you do, you won't be able to connect with passion and purpose with others.

When the COVID-19 pandemic hit, I was stuck home taking care of my young kids day in and day out. I became a full-time dad plus cooked, cleaned, did dishes, and helped with homeschooling. In the beginning, I found myself depressed, unhappy, and sneaking away to the bathroom multiple times an hour to check social media. After a month, I realized this COVID thing wasn't going away anytime soon. I needed something to fill my completely dry cup so I could pour into my kids.

I decided I wanted to fulfill one of my childhood dreams, which was to get onstage and compete in a men's bodybuilding competition.

Each day, I woke up early to prepare meals, work out hard, and practice posing for the show.

Each day, I was doing something for myself. In turn, I loved being home with my kids, and my kids loved being around me. I was able to be completely present for them. I loved that special time I was able to spend with them. I filled my cup so

I could pour into theirs. And after training for a year, I was able to fulfill my childhood dream.

Here are some daily routines I use to fill my cup.

- morning walk: wake up around 5:00 a.m. to go outside to be with myself before the house is awake
- weightlifting: thirty-five to forty-five minutes hitting the weights each day
- writing: one hour a day writing, five days a week
- reading: fifteen to thirty minutes a day reading books and at least forty-five minutes on audiobooks while driving the car or walking the dog
- cell phone limits: no cell phone use from 3:00 to 4:00 p.m. to allow me to be present for my kids
- coffee time: after completing a section of work, reward myself with coffee and sit alone with my thoughts

I recommend revisiting your needs and journaling about how to fill your cup daily so you can pour it into others.

Second Rung: Connection Eliminates the "Me Too" Experiences

Connecting is listening. If you are listening in order to respond, instead of listening to understand, you are more concerned about yourself than trying to build a connection.

One of the best ways to connect with others is to eliminate the phrase "me too" from your vocabulary. As in, that same situation happened to me. People believe that if they share a similar experience, it will connect you better to the other person. In fact, each time you say "me too" you take away from another's experience. It's challenging to allow someone to tell a story and be present in their story without thinking you want to share your similar experience.

Connecting is *not* gained by talking about a similar experience with someone who just trusted you with theirs. They poured into you only for you to come over the top of them to share your similar experience in hopes of building a relationship and inflating your ego.

Let another's story "be" without sharing yours.

One of my friends recently told me about how she met former President Bill Clinton while she was at a restaurant. She was utterly surprised when he walked in during a meal, thrilled to meet him. She eagerly recounted the entire experience, even sharing a photo they took together. Excitement radiated from her as she shared, and I, equally thrilled, asked for more details. I listened attentively, making the conversation all about her and her memorable encounter.

Now, I also met Bill Clinton, have a great story about my experience, and have a photo with him. If I had stopped or interrupted my friend to share my "me too" experience, that would have taken away from that moment for her. Sharing my experience would have diminished hers, leaving her feeling disconnected. Her story would lose its significance, drowned out by my own.

To go further in life, make it all about others.

A self-centered person talks about themselves.

A gossip is someone who talks about others.

A connector is someone who talks to you about yourself. Be a connector.

On the other hand, sometimes when telling a story and someone interjects, saying, "That happened to me too," it's extraordinary. Letting others share similar experiences fosters their connection with you. If building relationships, connections, and influence is your aim, permit others to have those moments while you observe and listen. Curb your own ego and witness the transformative impact on your world.

Often people believe they must talk about themselves in order to connect with others. When someone gets done with a story, they feel it's their opportunity to share an example of how something like this happened to them. Many times, the point is entirely different, and the person who originally shared their story typically feels like it was pushed under the rug. Realize it's not about you. The faster you do, the quicker you will connect with others.

Third Rung: Connection Is Eliminating "Should" from Your Vocabulary

Should = Advice

If they didn't ask for advice, don't give it.

Have you ever given someone advice? Told them what they should do? Very rarely will someone take your advice. Many times, they may even get mad at you for giving unsolicited advice.

When others tell you about their problems or even ask for your advice, most of the time they don't want to hear what you have to say.

When they're navigating their emotions, advising them on what they should do doesn't establish a connection; it feels more like directing. Nobody appreciates being told what to do. I understand you've experienced similar situations, and your intention is to assist your friend, but offering advice repeatedly results in frustration for both of you, hindering rather than helping. If you insist on commenting in hopes of helping, use the phrase, "you could," instead of saying, "you should." The word "could" eliminates the assumption you know better than them. You *could* suggests without directing and telling them what they "should" do.

> If you insist on commenting in hopes of helping, use the phrase, "you could," instead of saying, "you should."

I believe the word *should* is the worst word in the dictionary. It exemplifies that you know better and are more intelligent than the other person. You're saying, "Listen to me because I'm a professional, and you have so much to learn to catch up to me."

Most people have too much ego to realize you are trying to help. Curb your advice and lay off the "shoulds."

Example 1:
I wonder what to get my wife for her birthday.
"You *should* buy your wife flowers to celebrate her birthday."
Replace with:
"You *could* buy your wife flowers to celebrate her birthday."

The word *should* is a command. The word *could* is an invitation. How do you like to be asked to do something? Do you like to be commanded or invited? "Could" is a suggestion, and "should" is telling someone else how to be.

> *Example 2:*
> My head hurts.
> "You *should* try this new herb that worked for me."
> *Replace with:*
> "You *could* try this new herb that worked for me."

Do you see the transformation? It may not seem like much of a difference to you, but by becoming a "could" person, you cultivate strong connections. This approach enhances your relationships and overall well-being, making you more appealing for others to connect with.

Fourth Rung: Connection Does Not Mean Burdening Others

Talking about all of your problems with someone else creates a false sense of connection. You may unintentionally cause them to feel bad for you and feel like they need to check in with you later to ensure your well-being. You may need emotional support. You may need attention because you feel sorry for yourself. You may even be scared.

But after a while, you notice others distancing themselves from you. They don't want to hear everything that worries you anymore. They have their own worries and their own lives to tackle.

While it may seem delightful to have someone consistently listen, worry, and make you feel special, it can create the opposite effect. Building a strong relationship isn't achieved by making others feel sorry for you. Sharing that you need medical tests or are unwell is understandable as you navigate a challenging situation. However, consistently worrying others about it can erode the connection over time.

If you need to process something with a friend, do it and then move on until further details emerge. The more you concentrate your brain on the worries, the less time you have to be happy. This will shift your energy to a positive vibe instead of a negative one.

What is the point of having continuous worry in your life? All it does is create anxiety. It doesn't solve any problem. The anxiety you feed can even make you sicker.

On the other hand, if someone feels the need to share their concerns, listen attentively and allow them to express themselves because it will strengthen the connection. If you seek more from life, prioritize making it about others each time someone confides in you. Consider it an honor to be the chosen one, as they trust you with their worries. Be there for your friend, and in return, they may open a world of possibilities for you. Remember: connection is centered on others—just because someone shares their worries doesn't mean you should burden them with yours.

Fifth Rung: Connecting on Common Ground

Do you engage in debating others, hoping you can knock some sense into them and convince them to change their beliefs? Do you believe that your advanced education and champion communication skills alone can sway the entire population to adopt your viewpoint and create global harmony? The challenge is that we all see the world differently. We were raised differently, had different experiences, and grew up in different areas.

Influencing people doesn't come from convincing them their views are wrong; rather, it stems from initially establishing connections based on common ground.

I used to think that in order to convince and lead others, I needed to be the best. The fastest, the strongest, the wealthiest, and the smartest.

But connection isn't about superiority. It's emotional, not logical. If I talk to you about something that is important to me but insult you in the process, you won't have a good feeling about me, and it will hinder a positive connection.

In order to connect with others, finding similarities is a great start. It all begins where your interests, beliefs, and values intersect each other. By connecting on common ground, you allow the relationship to develop.

Furthermore, showing another person you genuinely care for and support them demonstrates a connection. When someone is pursuing goals, expressing interest and cheering them on signifies belief in their abilities. By investing love, time, knowledge, and resources, you contribute to their success. Building positive connections reflects a sincere desire for their success and well-being.

My friend Paul is the best salesperson I have ever met. He excels in sales because he goes over the top to genuinely care and see the good in everyone he meets. His profound care is evident in his sales, and it greatly contributes to his success. The money he makes is a by-product of what he is trying to accomplish.

One way he shows he cares is by asking questions. This approach provides insight, offers a welcoming environment, and contributes to engaging conversations. Instead of forcefully imposing beliefs, asking questions allows for an exchange of perspectives. When faced with a disagreement, try understanding the other person's viewpoint by asking questions. You might both be surprised by finding common ground instead of clashing.

Please Note...

Connections based solely on shared frustrations are temporary bonds, a connection trap. Discussing mutual grievances regarding spouses, bosses, politicians, or even the economy creates a limited connection, but once the frustration subsides, the relationship undergoes an abrupt transformation, leaving both parties separated, lost, and disheartened.

Initially, seeking to vent and clear your mind is natural. However, if you let negative emotions dominate your relationship through constant complaints, you inadvertently establish a false sense of connection, falling into the trap of superficial bonding.

If you find yourself going down the dark path of complaining, stop it. No good will come of it. Get to the root of the frustration and make the changes within yourself to build a strong, lasting connection—not one of gossip.

Opening My Mind to Opposing Views

I was struggling to find friends when our family moved nine years ago. I was surrounded by individuals with opposing political views, which led me to close myself off from the possibility of forming friendships with them.

One night I was invited to poker night with some dads from my children's preschool. My hope was to avoid discussing politics. Unfortunately, the game quickly transformed into a critique of my political side. Despite being educated on all the talking points to support the other side, the odds weren't in my favor. It was my first invitation anywhere since moving, and throughout the entire game, I bit my tongue as they delved into everything they saw wrong with my political party.

That night I gained a profound understanding. Despite having opposing political views, these individuals were genuine, caring human beings who were educated and far from the freeloaders the media and my social circle had portrayed them to be. Our initial perspectives on the world differed, but as more poker nights unfolded, friendships began to blossom around shared interests. They asked questions, discovered my opposing political stance, and to my surprise, our bond deepened. We built relationships based on commonalities, leading to our families even spending time together.

In the end, both sides gained an understanding of each other's views, and we all benefited from it. Our relationship grew stronger based on common ground.

Sixth Rung: Credibility Connects

If you commit to something, follow through. Don't promise something you can't deliver. There is no quicker way to fall down the rungs of the Connection Ladder than not delivering on a promise. Establishing credibility is challenging; it takes time and effort. It can be lost instantaneously by not doing what you say you will do.

It's no one's fault but your own if you forget, get overwhelmed, or get sidetracked. Others will not understand. You will immediately lose everything you've built. Your excuses will not matter.

If you need to break a promise, fess up and admit it as soon as possible. This gives you a fighting chance to make it up for it and keep your hard-earned connection.

If you're feeling overwhelmed, it's okay to say no. Don't fall into pressure; you don't have to commit to something that doesn't align with your capabilities or the expected timeline. Be honest and decline if you know it's not feasible for you.

Seventh Rung: Empowering Connection

The pinnacle of connection lies in empowering others to attain their envisioned potential. Giving the gift of empowerment establishes enduring connections and holds profound significance. Empowerment involves mentoring and contributing to someone's improvement. It stands as the utmost level of connection for a compelling reason. If your aim is to master the highest rung, wield boundless influence, and enrich relationships, then empower others. Reflect on what you can offer, and if your response is limited, consider your life's purpose. Without a clear answer, ponder what skills you can acquire and utilize to uplift others.

In high school, I wasn't the most diligent student, often receiving average grades. My primary interest was veering away from class, channeling my energy into extracurricular leadership roles. I enthusiastically handled morning announcements, organized fundraisers, participated in student council and peer leadership, and even took on the role of the school mascot. My senior year, I was honored with titles "Most School Spirit," "Done Most for the School," and "Most Helpful" by my peers.

My perspective on class changed when I encountered Mrs. Pomerantz. Unlike other teachers, she not only welcomed my company but took a genuine interest in my pursuits. She went above and beyond, actively supporting and empowering me to become better at my desired endeavors. This empowerment created a reciprocal effect; I worked harder for her. It was the magic of building a connection—she identified my interests, nurtured them, and in turn, I went out of my way to work harder in school, which ultimately led to my student ambassador scholarship at community college.

Mrs. Pomerantz understood the dynamics of empowerment and connection, earning my admiration. Her ability to tap into my potential made me dedicated and willing to work harder for her than anyone else. Her approach showcased the power of genuine connection and empowerment, leaving a lasting impact on me. It reshaped my perspective on building connections with others.

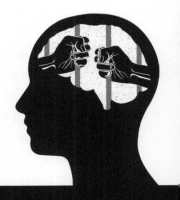

CHAPTER 10

BE GENEROUS

By giving, you are able to receive more than you already have.

Why should I bother helping them out? Nobody helped me when I was struggling.

WHAT IS YOUR purpose? When you're at the end of your life, will you be satisfied with how you lived?

I believe true life purpose is measured by the number of people you affect positively. The more people you positively impact, the more life fulfillment you are capable of having. Show me someone who gives, and I'll show you someone fulfilled.

I believe living once is more than enough; if you give everything you have, you will come to the end of your life with no regrets.

I believe if you spend the rest of your days working toward something real, like making a significant difference in the lives of others, you give yourself the best chance of reaching your potential.

How do you distribute your success? Do you hoard it or give it back? To live a growing, full life, you must give. Research consistently shows that acts of generosity, whether through time, resources, or support to others, can significantly contribute to one's overall sense of well-being and happiness. *You can be successful without giving, but you can't have fulfillment without giving.* Sharing your time, finances, or knowledge, and not expecting anything in return, is an unselfish act that makes the world a better place.

As you gain more success, you will have more means to magnify and help others even more. If you start giving now, you will gain momentum and build strong habits to have a more meaningful, fulfilled life. Anything worthwhile is achieved through others. Give the gift of giving.

> *"You will get all you want in life if you help enough other people get what they want."*
> —ZIG ZIGLAR

The world manifests success to those who give. Start now. Start where you are. Start giving. You may not have much to offer at this point, but as you give, more and more opportunities will present themselves, expanding your capability for generosity even more. In the beginning, you won't see the results of giving. Though as you continue to give, your life shifts and more personal and professional opportunities will come to you. This is the side effect of giving but should never be the motivating factor.

As the Business Networking International (a professional referral business group) slogan says, "Givers Gain." The more you give, the more you gain.

By hoarding success, you will never be satisfied. You will always be chasing and never have enough money, time, or satisfaction if you are constantly gathering instead of distributing. You may think you are building toward the future, but you are actually crippling your future.

Giving is *not* offering others unsolicited advice. As mentioned in chapter 9's Connection Ladder, giving unsolicited advice doesn't work.

Unsolicited advice tells others they aren't good enough the way they are and that you know better. People don't want your advice on what you believe is best for their situation. All your unsolicited advice may do is have them defend their egos or feel bad about themselves.

If you want to help someone, ask questions to guide them to reach their success. Questions help others gain awareness of themselves and open their mind to another way. Your questions give them the best chance to become aware of the changes they need to make.

Be careful when offering solicited advice. If someone asks for your advice, they do it for one of two reasons. Either they admire your opinion, or they need to talk out their problem. Most of the time, they aren't looking for advice. You will often hear someone say, "I would love your advice," but then they carry on talking with no clear sign of being open to considering a different way. The best thing you can do is become a good listener and ask questions to help them gauge what they need to do.

Giving is dedicating your time or finances to improve someone or something.

Dedicating a portion of your finances and/or time on an ongoing basis is a gratifying practice. There are many ways to spend your time or money to help others. Many nonprofits need help both financially and with volunteer hours.

Giving your time and/or money to others can foster a sense of community, empathy, and relationships. It contributes to building a more compassionate and supportive society, helping address the needs of those less fortunate, and creating a positive impact on the well-being of individuals and communities as a whole. Imagine what a world full of givers would look like. You can start giving now, and your actions will motivate the world around you.

> *Imagine what a world full of givers would look like.*

In order to affect the most significant number of people, you must continue developing yourself and pouring into others daily. Work harder on yourself than you work on anything else. As you develop yourself, you will have more opportunities to give to others. Growing yourself allows you to grow others.

> *"You cannot give what you do not possess."*
> —JOHN MAXWELL

I used to hoard my knowledge and skills. My thought process was to stay one step ahead of others by not sharing or giving anything that could benefit someone else. I was in constant competition with others, trying to inflate my ego and look better than I was. Deep down, I was scared of others advancing themselves further than me. I tried to rationalize a meaningless justification for why anyone else was more successful than me. I was physically working harder than anyone around me but wasn't as successful as them. I was grinding, not growing. I was working hard on what did not matter. I allowed my ego to get in the way of learning from others. I was a know-it-all.

What if you give to others, and they grow more than you?

If you help others grow, they could advance themselves further than you. That scared me because it could cost me a job, an employee, or a raise. I now realize that giving to others is the greatest compliment you can give. As you continue to advance yourself and others, there is no telling how many lives you will impact.

I didn't understand that giving allowed me to grow and become a better person than I was. Instead of giving, I spent my time on activities, socializing, and always looking to the next fun thing, but I failed to get ahead. I was in constant search of doing something that made me happy but was trapped because I wasn't becoming mentally better and learning the skills I needed to grow and ultimately give back.

> *"You can have everything in life you want if you just help others get what they want."*
> —ZIG ZIGLAR

Spend your time making others successful.

Give more than you receive.

List the people in your life. Are you primarily the giver or the receiver in each of those relationships? Do others do more for you than you do for them?

I used to be more of a receiver. I still receive a lot from others and am incredibly grateful for everything. However, if you allow others to give you more than you give them, you lose control over yourself. You fall into the traps of self-pity, frustration, and dissatisfaction. Your fulfillment is dependent on others doing for you.

It's never a good idea to keep score of who did more in any relationship, but if you give everything you have each day, eventually, you will have everything you want. People who keep score think they need to be appreciated more, and no matter what someone else does, the focus is on themselves instead of the other person. Their needs will always fall short of what others give. It's always nice to feel appreciated, but when your self-worth depends on it, you tailspin out of control.

How about not needing any appreciation? That sounds crazy to most of you, but your unmet needs are based on your inflated ego. If you are not feeling appreciated, you believe you deserve more. You need to feel a sense of worth. If you don't receive that validation, you want to put others down or reach out to someone who can inflate your ego.

How about doing the best you can and seeing the best in everyone?

Change to being a giver instead of a receiver in order to become what you want instead of what you are. Take back ownership of yourself by making it all about others.

Do you ask more of others, or do you do more for others?

Are you a taker and allowing others to give to you constantly? The more you allow others to do for you, the more power they have over you. Whether they want to or not, they own you.

I love receiving from others. When someone buys me dinner or helps me achieve something I want, it feels great and special. But if I allow another person to give to me and not give back, my self-fulfillment goes down, and my dependence goes up. If you are a constant taker, it will limit your growth. To change, start by taking ownership of your life and do things yourself instead of always needing help. Give back, and as you do, you will take ownership of yourself and control your destiny.

It's exhausting to always give to the same people. You might get frustrated with them or even create boundaries around them.

I love the saying, "You are who you spend the most time with." If you want to give yourself the best chance of reaching your potential, make your inner circle full of others with a giver's mindset.

So how can you attain a giver's mindset? By being receptive to learning, embracing failure, cultivating positivity, maintaining a beginner's perspective, and expressing gratitude. These qualities will enhance your potential for seizing opportunities and ultimately contributing more.

If you want to make a real difference in this world and build a life of significance, give the gift of giving.

Climb the rungs of the Giving Ladder.

THE GIVING LADDER

First Rung: Eliminate the Need for Recognition

Recognition makes us dependent on more recognition. Recognition inflates our ego and gives us a false sense of self-worth. I did not understand this concept for most of my life.

People love to have their egos stroked. It feels nice. But needing recognition is a never-ending trap. You never get enough of it.

Many people work toward accomplishing things just for the recognition. I fell into this trap many times, but others were able to see right through me.

I always looked for a pat on my back. I would say, "Look at what I did," or "Hunny, I took the trash out," looking for praise. I also would blast out to social media if I donated money to a charity.

It's great always to give, but doing it for the right reasons is essential. I donated to help those in need, but I was also doing it for the praise and to gain additional social media followers that came with it. There is a fine line between the right and wrong reasons.

Second Rung: Spend More Time on What Matters

People work so hard on planning a vacation or planning a four-course meal because it provides immediate gratification. Work hard on planning a vacation, and you have a great time for that moment. Work hard on a meal, and you and your family will be happy for that moment. These might be important to you. However, the more time and energy you spend on what doesn't matter, the less time you have for what does matter. Anything worthwhile takes consistent work. People love to work hard on what gives them more of an immediate result. But to have lasting gratification, you have to spend more time on yourself than you do anything else. Most give up when it gets difficult. By committing to growth, you no longer say, "Can I do this?" but "How can I do this?"

To reach your potential, you must refrain from pursuing immediate gratification. Think about anything worthwhile you have ever accomplished. It took work. It took failing at it, learning, adjusting, and failing some more until you finally had some success. Do this pattern over and over, and they will call you an overnight success. It's all about doing what is right repeatedly, and eventually, you can win.

I like to gamble. My game is roulette. Like all gamblers, we believe we have a system to win more often. But if I look at the history of my gambling, I think I am down. If I look at why I gamble, it is for instant gratification. If I pick the correct numbers consistently, I can win enough money to put that casino out of business, which is one of my ego-based dreams. Gambling gives me instant gratification. It is addictive. The more I do it, the more I want to do it again. To this day, I still like to gamble in Atlantic City, but only a couple of times a year, and I limit my time at the table. If I want lasting success, I must work on my future and not gamble with it.

Third Rung: Celebrate All Victories

How do you respond when you have a victory? Did you expect to win? Do you ignore the victory and move on to the next thing? Do you hide it because you don't want to make others jealous?

Remember: it's extremely important to celebrate all victories. Each time you celebrate, you release your happiness into the world, which boosts your confidence and motivation, promotes a positive environment, and strengthens resilience. Your wins become contagious. You are showing others what hard work, perseverance, and determination can result in. Others will want to emulate you, and your success and happiness will spread like wildflowers to your circle of followers. By celebrating, you give the gift of winning to others.

Many people bottle up victories because they don't want to make others jealous of their successes. They don't want to throw their amazing life into another's struggling face. But it's quite the opposite. Each time you celebrate, you are giving permission to feel good; others will want to feel that as well. If you are hearing about another's success, it means you are on the same wavelength. Keep learning, growing, actively adjusting, and taking action toward what you want, and your success will be inevitable. Celebrate all victories and cheer others on. It is only a matter of time before your attitude will ignite the flames for others in your pathway.

By holding in your victory, you are delaying happiness to another time. You may be waiting for the big victory to celebrate. But no one begins with a big victory. A big victory is gained through a bunch of small victories over time. Keep building and working toward the big victory as you celebrate the small ones. Imagine a world where everyone is achieving and nobody is grieving. That is a world where everyone celebrates victories and motivates others to kick-start them to where they want to go.

Celebration versus Bragging

Be careful not to brag when celebrating. Here is the difference.

Celebrating is:
- talking about an achievement without having to put another down in the process.
- sharing joy and achievements in a positive and inclusive manner.

- giving credit away. Your success wouldn't be what it is without others. Be humble and express gratitude for those who made your success possible.
- focusing on the accomplishment rather than oneself.
- creating a positive atmosphere, fostering camaraderie, and encouraging others.

Bragging is:
- the desire to highlight one's superiority or accomplishments for self-promotion.
- emphasis on the individual rather than the achievement. This creates resentment or discomfort in others, as it tends to emphasize personal success without considering the feelings of those around. Intentionally brings you praise or clout.
- doing it for some external credit. "Look how great I am."

In summary, celebrating is a positive and shared expression of joy and success, while bragging may involve a more self-centered and boastful approach that can potentially alienate others. It's important to be mindful of how our expressions impact those around us and to share achievements with humility and consideration.

I have fallen into this bragging trap many times. I would do a good deed, only to bring it up later for a pat on the back. Unconsciously, I was feeding my inflated ego. I needed to do that because I lacked self-worth. I did not realize it until it was brought to my attention.

Fourth Rung: Control Your Destiny

Do you depend on others in order to get through your basic daily tasks?

I was initially excited to get the new iPhone about seven years ago but quickly became frustrated as I needed to learn much more than my old phone. My wife already had the new iPhone and was extremely knowledgeable about using it. I was always asking her for help day after day. I refused to learn it on my own. I just wanted her to fix it. The problem was that I needed the phone for business, and the amount of ever-changing new stuff I needed to learn caused me to become impatient, easily frustrated, and resistant to any change. I needed her to fix my problems so I could be the person I was.

She never seemed to mind helping, but in the process, I couldn't take control of my own life. My identity relied upon her skills, and I wasn't in control of my own responsibilities.

I remember the breaking point. I took my cell phone and threw it down the stairs of my home out of frustration. I didn't want to learn, and I didn't want to have my life dependent on another person anymore.

Looking back, I can see how childish I had been. I didn't want my life controlled by her, but I was refusing to learn and refusing to change. I just wanted the world to hand me the knowledge I needed. I felt like I deserved it and was entitled to it.

When I finally took control of my life, I was no longer a weight holding Karen down. I was free to become the best version of myself.

Fifth Rung: Work Harder on Yourself Than Anything Else

What is your plan for retirement? Are you counting down the days? If you are like most people, you started talking about and planning for your retirement several decades in advance. You will have time for your hobbies, meeting up with friends, and travel. The idea of a continuous party sounds good to most of you. But, in life, there is no such thing as a finish line. If you're waiting for the magic retirement finish line, you probably will be disappointed when you realize you are only waiting around to die. You may say, "I worked hard my entire life. Shouldn't I be able to enjoy it when I retire?" If you continue to grow yourself every day, you are enjoying life every day. You wake up every morning excited to improve yourself to effectively impact others.

But each day you wake up to your retired life, you may be concentrating on your self-fulfillment. You begin playing *not to lose* instead of playing *to win*. Growing yourself focuses on winning and serving others. Self-fulfillment focuses on serving yourself and trying not to lose. Fulfillment is not a sustainable emotion. We all slip into different moods that positively or negatively impact our lives. But if you continually grow, your focus is always on improving. As you do, you will have more means to serve others. Fulfillment is the by-product of personal improvement. If you better yourself, you will always win, and in the process, you will have more means to give.

You can't take your hobbies and interests with you when you die, but by concentrating on self-development, you leave a mark on others. In my previous business, I built a routine that most people would be jealous of. Each workday, I made time for exercise, hitting a bucket of golf balls, sipping several cups of coffee, and leaving by 2:30 p.m. most days to pick up my kids from school. My focus was on self-fulfillment. After a while, I became bored and depressed with my routine. I wanted more. I'm so blessed to have been able to find personal development. Now I live my days by becoming better so I can have more resources to serve more people.

Sixth Rung: Don't Let Stuff Own You

Do you own your stuff, or does your stuff own you? Do you have a desire to acquire? Not letting material possessions or external circumstances define your happiness or self-worth is essential.

Often, people's self-worth is determined by what they own. They look at their possessions and see valuable products that boost their self-esteem. This way of thinking is flawed, because those physical items rarely give us the satisfaction we think they will. In fact, the items you own could very well be the liability holding you back from living on your terms.

We are all just passing through life, and our self-worth is not determined by how much we accumulate but by how many people we affect.

Seventh Rung: Give Empowerment

Giving to others so they can reach their desired success is called empowerment—enabling and supporting individuals to develop the confidence, skills, and resources needed to take control of their lives.

There are two ways to empower others. First, by giving them the skills you possess, and second, by sharing the resources you have.

You will reach the magic place of significance if you can consistently empower others. Significance is where you live each day asking, "How can I do good for the world today?" If you multiply helping and doing good for the world daily, you can take the journey toward significance. Significance is achieved by creating habits to consistently give to help others. It's all about others.

As I strive for significance, I ask myself each morning what I can do for others that day. In the evening, I then reflect on the day and look at how I could have improved.

As you embark on your personal growth journey, I hope you feel inspired and encouraged to embrace change, make yourself better, pursue your aspirations, and give to others.

True significance and fulfillment are gained by transforming each day into the best version of you while contributing to others and empowering them to reach their potential.

Well, there you have it. I hope my book inspires and empowers you to apply these principles to live your best life. By becoming the best version of yourself, you become the positive change this world needs while living in inner peace. Keep this book close by to refer to when you are challenged. Be patient with yourself and stick with it. As you begin to notice changes within, you will experience liberation and empowerment. I hope you feel inspired to change the world with me.

If you work on climbing the rungs of each chapter regularly, you will see a major difference in yourself, your relationships, and success.

I wish you fulfillment on your journey in life and hope *Character Evolution* can be the catalyst for growth and change.

ACKNOWLEDGMENTS

I want to express my heartfelt gratitude to my wife, Karen, without whom this book wouldn't have come to fruition. Throughout this journey, she took on various roles, some unexpected and many unwanted, yet she wore each hat with grace. From playing devil's advocate to being the editor and more, she contributed in countless ways. We spent months brainstorming ideas, engaging in debates until they felt just right. Thank you for being yourself. I love you.

I extend my gratitude to Dr. Brett Caminez, my accountability partner and dear friend. Our weekly phone calls have been instrumental in keeping me on track, clearing away life's challenges. I look forward to our calls and value your guidance. Your support and keeping me focused played a crucial role in bringing this book to life. Thank you.

A special thank you to Alan Miner-Berger for reading through my work, offering encouragement, and assisting with my writing style. Beyond that, your character has contributed to shaping the person I am today. I'm grateful for you.

To John Maxwell, whose influence set me on the path of personal growth and leadership. You've been instrumental in shaping my journey, and for that, I'm forever grateful. Your books, which I read repeatedly, serve as my guiding light when I'm stuck, providing the answers I need.

To my children, Tenley and Trent, may this book serve as a reminder of the rewards that come from hard work, passion, and determination. I love you both deeply, and I believe you have much to offer the world. My greatest wish for you is to pursue whatever brings you joy and fulfillment.

I'm grateful to Roddy Galbraith for equipping me with the necessary tools I need to craft a compelling narrative.

Thanks to Karen Seeman for opening my mind to a new way of thinking.

Thanks to my parents and brother, Matt, for the life experiences during my upbringing that have brought me to where I am today. The lessons I've learned from those experiences are invaluable, and I wouldn't have been able to write this book without them. Extremely grateful for the lessons and the journey.

Finally, thank you to God for accepting and forgiving my sins. I look forward to building a stronger relationship with you.